# PEDRO ARRUPE, SJ

# PEDRO ARRUPE, SJ

## HIS LIFE AND LEGACY

## GEORGE BISHOP & LUCIEN LONGTIN, SJ

## GRACEWING

Originally published as
*Pedro Arrupe, S.J. Twenty-Eighth General of the Society of Jesus*
by Gujarat Sahitya Prakash, India and Gracewing, England in 2000,
revised edition published by Gracewing in 2007

This condensed edition published in 2021
by
Gracewing
2 Southern Avenue
Leominster
Herefordshire HR6 0QF
United Kingdom
www.gracewing.co.uk

ISBN 978 085244 969 1

Typeset by Gracewing
Photographs from the life of Father Arrupe,
Courtesy the General Curia of the Society of Jesus, Rome

Cover design by Bernardita Peña Hurtado

# CONTENTS

# ACKNOWLEDGEMENTS

FR. Longtin wishes to express his deep gratitude to Dr. Harry Rissetto, to Deacon Chris May, to Rev. Robert Wiesenbaugh, S.J., to Fr. Herb Keller, S.J., to Fr. Dave Sauter, S.J., and to Rev. Frank Kaminski, S.J. for all the work they put into proofing this text and helping to arrange its publication with the gracious compliance of Gracewing Publishing. He wishes also to thank the family of the original author, the late George Bishop: Mr. Bishop's dear wife Dawn and their son, Rev. Simon Bishop, S.J., for permitting Fr. Longtin, S.J., to adapt Mr. George Bishop's wonderful biography of Fr. Pedro Arrupe, S.J. for reading by high school and early college students.

# Prologue

W HAT FOLLOWS IN this book is an updated and abbreviated version of a scholarly and splendid biography of Rev. Pedro Arrupe, S.J. written by the late George Bishop and published originally by Gujarat Sahitya Prakash, India and Gracewing, England in 2000, with a revised edition published by Gracewing in 2007.

This new version is intended to make that biography accessible and interesting for high school students and perhaps for college students too. It omits and revises certain sections of George Bishop's wonderful original and carefully researched account of Fr. Arrupe's life, those sections which would have less interest for high school students.

This revision has retained much of the original writing, omitting only segments that the editor thought be of less interest, and entering at times summaries to convey briefly important portions of Fr. Arrupe's life. He shows the way to greatness for us all: service, prayer, and humble compassion.

Fr. Longtin feels that anyone who becomes as enthralled by the person and the life of Fr. Arrupe as he is, owes a huge debt of gratitude to George Bishop for the invaluable work done by him in making known crucial features of Arrupe's life and Jesuit ministry. Arrupe was a great man and a great and holy Jesuit, and Bishop has helped to show why.

# 1 A DECLARATION OF WAR

I T WAS 5:00 a.m. That was the time Pedro Arrupe always got up. He put his feet on the *tatami* (straw) mat beside his *futon* (bed). He stepped across the wooden floor towards the rice-paper window. He opened it. A draught of cold air blew in, carrying the smell of the sea. It was still dark. It was a typical winter morning in Japan, cold and dreary and drizzling. He could hear the melancholy pattering of the rain on the tin roof. Otherwise it was quiet. There was no bird song, which was often a feature of early mornings at other seasons of the year. Occasionally the quiet was broken by the hoot from one of the deep-sea fishing vessels at the port of Yamaguchi.[1]

Pedro Arrupe was the assistant parish priest of Yamaguchi. Father Domenzain, the parish priest (pastor) had gone to Spain to raise funds; so, in effect Father Arrupe was the acting pastor. He had been there for two years. Ever since his days as a novice Jesuit, he had dreamed of being a missionary in Japan, like the great apostle of the East, Saint Francis Xavier. And here he was, in the very parish where the great saint began his work.

He closed the window and sat down at his desk. A bed and two chairs were the only other furniture in the room. He opened his Breviary. He flicked the pages. It was December 8, the Feast of the Immaculate Conception of the Blessed Virgin Mary. He began reading:

---

[1]   *Yamaguchi*, a region of plateaus and hills, is at the extreme south-west of Honshu Island, bordered on the north by the Sea of Japan, the Shimonoseki Strait to the southwest and the Inland Sea to the south. It was here that the European trading vessels came four hundred years earlier. Yamaguchi was then the prefectural capital, dating from the fourteenth century and once the capital of Japan and the residence of the Imperial Family. The town had once prospered under the Ouchi feudal lords. It had been built in 1350 after the style of the city of Kyoto. It was now a fairly large city of 30,000 inhabitants. It was a friendly city, neither industrial nor commercial, seemingly surviving on a distinctive aristocratic history and culture, independent somehow of money.

Father, You prepared the Virgin Mary to be the worthy mother of your Son. You let her share beforehand in the salvation Christ would bring by His death, and kept her sinless from the first moment of her conception ...

---

The young priest, thirty-four years old, stopped his reading as the patter of bare feet running across the floorboards reached his ears.

"Father!" a voice cried out.

An elderly face, crumbling up like paper, with a pointed goatee beard, peered round the door. It was old Michael Saito. He was one of the stalwarts of the parish. He bowed, exposing the full view of his head, completely bald, with just one long tress that hung down his back. His brown wrinkled eyes were excited.

"Father, have you heard?" he asked breathlessly.

"Heard what?" Father Arrupe answered.

"We are at war!"

Pedro could not believe his ears.

"Yes Father, war. It was on the wireless."

That news was beyond Arrupe's belief. "War!" he said to himself as he got up from his chair. "War? ...You mean the Americans have attacked Japan."

"No, Father. The Japanese have attacked America."

This was even more incredible.

They made their way to the parish hall. A group of people had already assembled there. They were huddled around a *hibachi* (charcoal stove), listening to a crackling radio:

This is an announcement from His Imperial Majesty's Government:

This morning at 7:55 a.m., the Armed Forces of His Imperial Majesty attacked the Grand Fleet of the United States of America anchored at the U.S. Naval Base of Pearl Harbor, Honolulu. The attack has been a brilliant success. Our Forces have destroyed the entire battleship fleet of the United States. All our aircraft have returned safely to their bases. This action was taken by His Imperial Majesty's Government to counteract the continued conquests in the East of the imperialist powers of the United States and Great Britain. From this moment this country is at war. We shall fight till all the subjugated peoples of the East have been fully liberated.

A contributory factor for Japan's recourse to war was its overpopulation. The density of population was one thousand inhabitants per square kilometer of habitable land. One solution of the problem was to acquire more land—by conquest.

But there was one obstacle to the Japanese ambitions—the United States Navy. If it could be eliminated in one sudden attack, while it slept peacefully at Pearl Harbor, 'the effete Americans' would be neutralized, and Asia liberated. Which is what Japan did.

On November 26th of 1941, an attacking fleet of six aircraft carriers and accompanying cruisers were ordered to meet in unfrequented waters off the Kurile Islands, north of the Japanese archipelago. The date for an attack on Pearl Harbor was set by Admiral Yamamoto as Sunday, December 7. Under Admiral Nagumo, the fleet left the rendezvous point. Sailing secretly through the winter mists, the fleet headed for Hawaii and finally waited 272 miles north of Pearl Harbor.

On Sunday, December 7, 1941, at 7:55 a.m. (American Hawaii Time) 360 aircraft with support hunter fighters attacked the sleeping American fleet of 94 boats. Eight armor–plated battleships came into view. Under the eyes of the experienced Japanese pilots, the dive-bombers and torpedo planes unleashed their deadly cargo on the unsuspecting craft.

The damage inflicted was horrendous. In the first assault, three battleships were destroyed—the 'West Virginia,' the 'Oklahoma,' and the 'Arizona.' Another battleship capsized. One hour later, a second assault was launched. Heavy damage was inflicted on the battleships 'Nevada,' and 'Pennsylvania' and three destroyers were reduced to wrecks. By 10:00 a.m., the battle had ended. The U.S. Navy casualties amounted to 2,718 (2,000 dead); the U.S. Army casualties were fewer than 600 (200 dead). The Japanese casualties were less than 100 men, 20 planes, and five midget submarines. The U.S. battleship fleet had been destroyed. The U.S. aircraft-carrier fleet would have suffered a similar disaster but for the fact that it was on maneuvres at sea. The dominion of the Pacific was now in Japanese hands. "The world balance," as Winston Churchill recorded later in his Memoirs, 'had changed.'

Fr. Arrupe returned to his room. He flopped into his chair. He stared at the lone crucifix on the bare white wall in front of him, trying to comprehend the news he had just heard: WAR!

He had come from the United States of America to Japan in 1938 and it was now Japan, his new home, that had declared war on America, where he had been recently living for some years while he was completing his studies in theology. He recalled his first arrival in Japan. On September 30, 1938, he had set off from Seattle, on the West Coast of America for Yokohama. On the calm days, it was only if you watched the foam and spray at the stern of the ship that you realized that it was moving. He spent the monotonous days reading, praying, and chatting, showing his faith and his optimism. One bright morn, with the sea and the sky an incredible aquamarine, they saw in the distance the port of Yokohama. They entered the Bay of Tokyo. The ship finally anchored.

It was October 15. His first dawn in Japan, his long wait of ten years had come to an end. It was one of the few times he cried as a man. The first time was at the death of his father. The second was his farewell to the prisoners in the maximum-security prison in New York.

The phalanx of khaki-colored cranes rose up on the docks like giant seahorses raising their heads into the sky. His gaze looked fixedly at the first Japanese houses he could see. The porters were speaking Japanese. He begged the Lord to keep alive in him this fire for his adopted country, Japan. He took the train from Yokohama to Tokyo. He thought the men in navy-blue trousers and dark jackets, wearing pointed hats with initials were railway workers. They were, in fact, university students. He took in the mass of faces, the high cheek bones, the small noses and the very short hair, all impenetrable in their smiles and gestures. A whistle told them the train had arrived in Tokyo, the great city of six million inhabitants, the seat of the Emperor still held in great reverence. The crowded suburbs of wood, the noisy streets, the peculiar exotic music didn't impress Arrupe.

The first few months in Japan were confusing and perplexing, with the different language, the different habits and customs, the different food. Breakfast was usually bean-paste soup, rice with flakes of seaweed, green tea and if he was lucky, a sweet-bean pastry. He remembered the first serving of *kombu* soup. It took him all his time to swallow a few spoonfuls. The cook had asked him how he liked it. "Interesting," he replied. She knew what he meant. For seven consecutive days, she served him with *kombu* soup. After four days, he admitted he had come to like it.

Tamura-San, the cook was a widow with three children. She cooked and looked after the *shimpu samas* (priests). She was very holy with one foot on earth, the other in heaven. She was a daily communicant and recited the rosary each day. One day breakfast was late. The two Jesuits found her in ecstatic prayer before a statue of Buddha. The two were shocked.

"What are you doing?" one of them asked.

"Oh, I am praying," she replied.

Arrupe would often talk with Tamura-San to improve his conversational Japanese.

Like many a missionary before him, he suffered from 'culture shock.' He met a lady at her home. "Come upstairs," she said.

It was some time before he realized that this invitation was the same as the invitation "Come in." This was because the ground floors of the houses in Japan are a little raised. He visited his first Japanese house. He left his shoes—as was the Japanese ritual—on the stone hallway and went up the wooden stairs to a very clean room which was bare. This was because all the belongings and furniture were folded away till needed behind the folding sliding doors or stored in the cupboards.

An American family arrived in Yokohama and stayed in a Japanese hotel. They were perplexed to find no furniture. Eventually they opened the cupboards in which were stored the beds. Next day the waiter came down to their room. But there was no sign of anyone. He opened the cupboard. There he found them, in the bed—in the wardrobe cupboard!

Even the Japanese bath had its own ritual. The Japanese bath is double the height of a European bath but only half the length. One sits in it, cross-legged, in Japanese style, with the water, at an almost unbearable temperature, reaching up to the neck. All the family use the same bath and the same water. But before stepping into the bath, they will sponge and wash themselves clean. A foreign priest once stayed fifteen days with a family. Each evening the bath was prepared with clean, steaming water. But not knowing the custom, the priest would wash himself in the bath. He was very mortified when he later learned his mistake and realized he had deprived the family of its bath for the duration of his stay.

Arrupe's ears swam with the strange sounds of this incredibly difficult language—possibly the most difficult in the world. His head spun trying to decipher the syntactic gymnastics with so many different meanings, depending on how the word was pronounced. He found it difficult to jump from languages like English, French, German, or Spanish, which have a certain common skeleton, to a language truncated, polysyllabic, with inflexions which bore no relation even to Chinese, which is monosyllabic and without inflexion. Without assimilating the culture and without speaking the language, there was no possibility of preaching Christianity. Still he persevered as many missionaries before him had done. He volunteered to help out with any job. He offered to celebrate Mass with Fr. Hubert Schiffer, a German Jesuit who was working with Korean dock workers, at the house of one of them. They made their way along small side streets to the district of Fuchi. They stopped outside a small dirty house, in a sordid environment.

"Is this it?" Arrupe asked.

Fr. Hubert opened the sliding door. They entered a tiny room, dark and full of smoke. They opened the windows to let out the smoke. A few people were waiting in the room. They began setting up the altar. The people seemed indifferent; they certainly lived in dire poverty. Fr. Arrupe recalled how he "felt his soul fall to his feet." Was this the Japan he had dreamed of for so many years?

After Mass, he asked Fr. Schiffer: "Is all of Japan like this?"

"No," Fr. Hubert replied. "The Japanese are not like this, inside or out. These people are not Japanese. They are Koreans, poor abandoned immigrants, exiles, second-class citizens, who have their fingerprints taken, who are marginalized by the opulent Japanese society."

In the evening, he would have long chats with Fr. Hubert, who was Director of a Settlement Project in Tokyo, a huge house, more like a military camp. During the day, it was used as nursery for children whose mothers worked; in the afternoon and evening it became a night-school for adults. University students also participated in the 'social experiment.' He had been very impressed with these young men. He observed how they would sit on their *tatamis* (mats). They would first kneel on the *tatami* and then sit back to their heels. The Japanese could sit for hours like this. But for a westerner it was torture. Fr. Arrupe could never figure out which pained more—the knees or the heels.

One day, while still studying the language and the culture of Japan, he set out for Mount Fujiyama, 30 km. from Tokyo, a white extinct volcano which had erupted eighteen times up until the *Meijo* period (1707). It was not just a mountain, it was the Japanese Mt. Olympus, a divinity. Women were forbidden to climb it. One could travel on horseback up the mountain for the first 2,000 meters. Then it was by foot. Arrupe, accompanied by a religious brother, Moses Domenzain, set off at midnight so as to reach the summit before 4 a.m. After 6 o'clock the clouds set in. As the dawn sun met his eyes, at a height of 3,776 meters, the highest point in Japan, as the wind stirred his red vestment, he offered the Eternal Father the sacrifice of the Eucharist for the conversion of the 80 million people below him who did not know of the Savior.

In mid-1940, after 18 months of learning the language and the customs of the Japanese, Arrupe packed his suitcase and caught a train to Ube, an industrial city near Hiroshima, where he was to continue his work of social acculturation. But no sooner was he in Ube than he received an order to go immediately to Yamaguchi, the former parish of St. Francis Xavier, set in a valley surrounded by green mountains, 140 kilometers from Hiroshima.

It was now getting dark. The small congregation had gathered in the Yamaguchi church for the evening service in honor of the Feast of the Immaculate Conception. Fr. Arrupe was in the sacristy, getting his vestments ready for Mass. He suddenly became aware of loud banging on a door, of voices raised, of running footsteps thudding along the floor of the corridor. He opened the door. In the doorway stood the breathless, stocky figure of Kim, a Korean, who often acted as sacristan at the mission.

"Father! The *Kempeitai* are here," he managed to blurt out. "They have orders to search the premises."

The *Kempeitai* were the all-powerful Japanese military police, expert in all manner of torture, who could extract any secret from the most obstinate of persons.

Fr. Arrupe, smiling as usual, went out to greet his visitors. In the aisle of the church, he met them. An officer in jackboots, of bigger build than the average Japanese, clasping the hilt of his Samurai sword in his left hand, confronted him.

"Pedro Arrupe?" he inquired.

"Yes," the Spanish priest answered.

"We have orders to search the premises."

The few old men and women sitting in the pews waiting for the Mass to begin looked on in awe-struck bewilderment. Not for long. The police-soldiers ordered them out of the building. They shuffled out as fast as their tired, old legs would take them. Within the hour the entire Catholic community of Yamaguchi—or just about 100 people—had learned what had taken place. Was this, they wondered, the beginning of another persecution of the Church by the nationalist rulers who had just taken Japan into war?

The soldier began their search. They were most meticulous, not missing the smallest millimeter.

"What's this?" a soldier cried out. He had seen the gold-plated tabernacle and opened it.

"Please don't touch that," Fr Arrupe cried out as he rushed forward to the soldier now holding the ciborium in his hands. "Please put it down," he repeated as he ran up the altar steps.

Another soldier, suspecting trouble, rudely barred his way, rough-handling him in the process. Arrupe's natural reaction was to retaliate. However, he remembered the action of John Fernandez, a Spanish Brother who had been a companion of St. Francis Xavier. When in June 1587, some ruffian had spat in his face, his patient tolerance later won the conversion of a Japanese nobleman.

Kim, who had been standing back at a respectful distance behind his priest, rushed up to the guard. He shouted in his strange Korean accent, his arm raised.

A rifle butt in the midsection of the young Korean sent him sprawling, doubled up in agony. There was little love between the Japanese and the Koreans.

The Captain came forward and stood over the Korean. "*Keto* (barbarian)! You keep out of this or you too will be under arrest."

The word "too" was not lost on Fr. Arrupe.

The Captain took the ciborium out of the soldier's hands. "What's this?" he asked Fr. Arrupe, staring down at the white wafers.

"This is the body of Christ," Pedro Arrupe replied.

The Captain's eyes narrowed, the skin at the corners of the eyes creasing up like crinkled paper. The lines on his forehead cut deep furrows as he frowned. He just looked at Arrupe. The words were beyond his understanding and comprehension, as, indeed, they are to many today. He kept staring at Arrupe. Finally, he asked, "It is something of your religion, is it?"

The priest nodded.

What's this?" the Captain asked, picking up a somewhat fat leather-covered book, its pages lined with gold edging.

"That's my Breviary."

The Captain obviously didn't understand.

"I use it to say my Office."

"Office! Office!" the Captain murmured rapidly. "That was it," he thought," ... the office—that is where there will be any incriminating documents."

The Captain stopped the search of the church and made his men begin the search of the house. He pulled open a drawer. A large batch of letters faced him, all carefully catalogued. The Captain began to go through them. There were letters written in Spanish, some in Italian, some in German, some in English from America, a few even in Latin. This is what he wanted. Here was the proof he was looking for, proof in writing of Arrupe's involvement in some international, political espionage-ring.

Before Arrupe could explain that the letters were from his friends in various parts of the world, the Captain had placed the letters in his briefcase. "You will come with me to Military-Police Headquarters."[2]

It was cold outside. The snow was beginning to fall silently on the already white pavement. A cold wind blowing from the sea made it very cold. He turned up his collar to protect himself. He was bundled unceremoniously into a waiting van and driven off.

At the military-police headquarters, Arrupe was made to wait a long time while the authorities checked his letters and papers. A soldier with a rifle off his shoulder kept watch. Finally he was led into a room. Seated at a table were three men. He was made to stand before them.

"Why am I being held here?" Pedro Arrupe asked.

The man in the middle of the trio scowled angrily through the thick lenses at the impudence of the question.

"You know very well. You have been caught. We have been watching your activities for several months. You are a Western spy and this proves it," he said as held up some of Arrupe's letters. He almost spat out the word "spy," exposing pink gums below teeth yellow from tobacco smoke.

"A spy!" Arrupe laughed at the suggestion.

"You are a spy and a saboteur. You have been undermining our war preparations."

---

[2]    At the best of times, foreigners were looked on with some suspicion by the nationalist government—especially those, such as Arrupe, who enjoyed considerable popularity with people of all beliefs and all ranks. The Catholic Church was considered very anti-Japanese, as against the *kokutai*, (the national policy). It was now war. A foreign priest was especially suspect.

The Spanish priest was flabbergasted. "Spy! Saboteur! Sabotage! What sabotage?"

You have been preaching *heiwa* (peace) to your parishioners.

This was true. Fr. Arrupe was always advocating love and peace, denouncing war and violence.

"Of course, I have been preaching *heiwa* (peace)," he admitted.

"To talk of peace in time of war is sabotage," the interrogator replied. "We cannot have Western foreigners poisoning the minds of our brave young people with talk of peace."

"It is true," Arrupe went on, "sometimes war can be justified in self-defense, for example."

"That's right," the Captain shouted, as his *kimochi* (bad humor) increased. "We are defending ourselves against the American and British imperialists."

"But it is you who have attacked the Americans," the priest pointed out. "That is not self-defense."

The man glowered at the captive figure before him, the blue lines of his veins protruding from his thick bull neck. "We are fighting for justice," the officer continued, banging the table for added emphasis. "We are fighting to liberate Asia from Western imperialists like Britain and the United States. We are fighting to return Asia to the Asian peoples. This is our duty."

The man was obviously completely convinced of the rightness of his cause.

The interrogation continued through the night.

"A letter from Germany. How do you explain that?"

"I was invited to read a paper at a medical conference in Vienna."

"You are a medical doctor then?" he asked.

Arrupe nodded.

"These letters from America. How do you explain them?"

"They are from friends in America. I was sent to the United States to complete my studies."

"But you could have completed your studies in Spain, where you were born and educated. Why should you go to the United States? Perhaps at the behest of American intelligence?"

Arrupe shook his head, laughing derisively at such a ridiculous suggestion.

"I wouldn't laugh if I were you, the interrogating officer pointed out sternly, nodding his head as he said so. "So why did you leave Spain?"

"I was expelled from Spain."

"Expelled!" A wry smile came over the questioner's face. "What crime did you commit?" he asked, turning to his companions on either side in self-congratulation. He could feel himself tying the knot of guilt tighter and tighter around the priest.

"I didn't commit any crime. The anti-Catholic socialist government of the time expelled all Jesuits from the country."

The three men consulted among themselves. They decided to charge Arrupe with espionage. He would be held in *Yamaguchi's* maximum-security prison for political prisoners and others considered a danger to the State.

It was early in the morning when he was led out of the Military Headquarters. The pale orange light was trying to make its presence felt through the mist and the fog. It was bitterly cold. He pulled up the collar of his coat. Across the road, he could see a group of silent onlookers. They were members of his parish who had waited up all night outside the military headquarters to get news of their much-loved priest. They watched in disbelief as Father Arrupe was rough handled into an open van and driven away to prison like a common felon.

## 2 Solitary Confinement

THE TRUCK WOUND its way over the dirt track towards *Yamaguchi* prison. Little streams from the rain had formed in the road. There was a smell of sea and trees and mud and hens and cows and horses and manure. In the distance, immense limestone outcroppings could be seen on the plateau, gently covered in a mantle of light snow. Yamaguchi was famous for its limestone and marble caves. The rice-fields and the mandarin-orange groves also were covered in white. From the vessels in the port twists of black smoke curled up into the dull gray sky.

The truck lurched from side to side as the vehicle bumped its way over the dirt-road. Whenever the truck slowed or stopped, little knots of curious bystanders stared at the unusual sight of a *gaijin* (foreigner) being taken off in police custody. Fr. Arrupe was placed in a conspicuous position in the back of the open truck so that he could be easily seen as he was paraded through the streets as a felon. The people had their collars turned up against the cold.

As they neared the town, the ramparts of the castle were clearly visible. From *tenshu* (the tower), in the shape of a pagoda, fluttered the flag of the rising sun. The traffic grew in volume as they neared the town center; more and more vehicles, and cycles by the hundreds. The crowds, too, were thicker. They stared at the *gaijin* prisoner as if he were some strange animal in a zoo. There were young men shouting "*banzai!*"; there were older people too, with sunken cheekbones, their backs bent like drawn bows. A *samurai* wearing a large black umbrella-like hat, had his hand on a long sword hanging near the loose sleeves of his garment. A *bonze* (Buddhist monk) stopped chanting his sad *sutra* as he watched the strange scene. The truck deliberately went into the market-place, where the crowds were denser, the more to embarrass the priest.

They passed the Memorial Park flanked by tall pines to guard it from evil spirits, which would get entangled in the pine needles. The magnolias and wisteria were no longer in bloom. Arrupe used to come sometimes to stroll in this Park, over the meticulously raked gravel, representing the sea, dotted with occasional boulder to represent an island. Near the teahouse, shaped like a pagoda and surrounded by hostas and yakushimanum rhododendrons, clear water (now frozen) would tumble over a miniature waterfall and under tiny humpback bridges built in zigzag fashion to thwart the devil who "could only travel in straight lines." Arrupe wondered: "Would he ever enjoy such walks again?"

The truck finally stopped at the prison. The maximum-security jail was an old wooden house in which 30 to 40 prisoners were incarcerated. Fr. Arrupe knew the place from his visits to some of the inmates. He was surprised to see some of his parishioners waiting outside the gate for his arrival. News of his arrest had travelled fast. He was pleased to see them but sad at the circumstances. They stood silent, disbelieving, their mouths agape. Some women had their hands to their mouths. In front stood the elderly John, his head bowed, holding his flat cap in his hand, like the peasant in Millet's famous painting *The Angelus*. In his younger days, John would serve at the Mass. Next to him stood Sister Angela, with black rosary beads like a girdle around her habit, holding by the hand, two of her charges from the orphanage.

Without any courtesy or consideration, Fr. Arrupe was bundled out of the truck and led through the prison gates. He looked up at the sky. Was this the last time he would see it? He was given a rough prison uniform to wear—coarse black trousers and a grey striped shirt. He was shoved into a cell, 25 meters by 15. He heard the door clang behind him. He couldn't see a thing. He was enveloped in darkness like coal tar. After some time, he was able to make out the confines of his cell. There was no chair or table, just a dirty straw mat (*tatami*) on the hard stone floor, a metal receptacle in the corner. The marks on the wall were bloodstains.

So began his solitary confinement.

The words of St. Matthew provided some solace: "Blessed are you when men revile you and persecute you and utter all kinds of evil against you falsely on my account. Rejoice and be glad, for your reward is great in heaven; for thus men persecuted the prophets who were sent before you." (Matt. 5:11–12)

Arrupe later described his first night, a very long one: "The sun goes to bed at four o'clock and wakes fourteen hours later. There was no *futon* (bed); so I curl in the corner on a *tatami* (mat), trying not to worry. It was very cold. One could not sleep; I was shivering and my teeth chattering. At intervals, I got up to do Swedish gymnastics, so as to get warm. I pass a miserable night. At dawn, the cold sunshine appears through the window. There is absolute silence. The hours pass with the increased slowness of waiting."

Ever the optimist, he hoped to celebrate Mass that day. But there was no sign of life anywhere. As the morning wore on, he realized there was little chance of that happening. He leaned out of his cell and spoke to a passing guard. The guard made it clear he was going to be there for a long time and that instead of worrying about Mass, he should be worrying about food. Later that day, the cell door clanged open; a warder, his face red from drinking too much *sake*, passed him a bowl of turnip leaf soup.

The warder didn't speak. It was obvious he regarded the *gaijin* (foreigner) with contempt and hatred. Christians were frowned upon; they were discredited as traitors to the nationalist cause.

Arrupe saw no one. He just got his bowl of soup. After two days, his cell door was violently swung open and twenty soldiers squeezed into the room. They were thickset men from the country, without any education or culture. They trod about the room in their heavy boots with the arrogance of soldiers who only know triumph. They pushed him into a corner and then started making partitions, confining him to an area of two meters on each side. This was to be his cell; he would be in solitary confinement, for how long he did not know.

The next day, he had a visitor: an interrogating officer. He was not the kind of person one would take to. As Arrupe later wrote, "He never looked you in the face, but kept looking at his reflection in the window." He put his papers on a table, hastily brought in, sat down, and then began asking Fr. Arrupe everything about his life—his name, his parents' names, where he was born, when, where he went to school, where he worked, everything. Arrupe answered the questions slowly and courteously.

———◆———

His name was Pedro Arrupe. He was born in Bilbao, in northwest Spain, on November 14, 1907. His family was not wealthy, but they were not poor. His father, Marcellino Arrupe, an architect, was the founder, along with other prestigious citizens, of the Catholic journal *La Gaceta del Norte*, one of the premier journals in Spain. His mother was Dolores Gondra. She was the daughter of a Basque doctor, one of six children. On the day he was born, the streets rang with shouts of "a son, a son!" At last, the family had a son. Pedro was the youngest in a family of four sisters: Catalina, Maria, Margarita, and Isabel.

It was the end of 1907. That was the year when Britain, France and Russia formed the Triple Entente to counter the triple alliance of Germany, Austria-Hungary and Italy. In South Africa, a little man, an Indian, with round glasses—Mahatma Gandhi—began the movement of passive resistance in favor of human rights. That year, the move for Women's Suffrage began in the United States. Lenin was expelled from the Soviet Union for the second time. In that year also, Gustav Mahler put music to the words of Goethe's *Faust*, in his great Symphony #8. Rudyard Kipling was awarded the Nobel Prize for Literature.

The next day, the infant was baptized by Fr. Gochica in the Basque Basilica of San Pedro, which still preserves its 14th century chapel, with its Gothic Renaissance door a few steps from the Arrupe home. As the priest poured water over the little head, he did not realize that head would bring the faith to thousands of people, that it would travel round the world several times, that it would speak fluently six languages—Spanish, English, French, German, Italian, and Japanese—and would command a weaponless army of 30,000 Jesuits.

It was a happy family that grew up in a second-floor apartment in No. 7 Pelota Street, with its eight spacious bedrooms, its large dining room and kitchen and balcony. Often the round smiling face of young Pedro would peer out the large windows, looking over old Bilbao, grand and busy, with old sunburnt men, with their typical Basque noses and wide shoulders, playing pétanque in their black berets. On the right side of the river Neivion, with boats crossing its dark-green, almost black water, stood tall dark houses. Smoke from chimneys climbed to the skies. Industrial Bilbao, with its steel factories, had begun to encroach on the old, tranquil town on the left side of the river.

He adored his father, a tower of security, tall, distinguished, his large moustache adding to the distinction. He remembered how his father would show him the cross of St. Andrew on the shield of Gondra and proudly tell how his ancestors had fought in the battles. He adored, too, his mother, tall, broad, firm but kind, ever serene and smiling, with deep penetrating eyes, always dressed in dark colors. He recalled jumping down the stairs, two at a time, to go and play in the park with his sisters, laughing and joking—they in their round hats and lace collars and he in a sailor suit with its wide, white rectangular collar edged with blue.

For holidays, the family would go to the coastal town of Algorta, with its unmistakable Basque charm, sheltering in a bay in the Cantabrian Sea. The beach would be lined with boats of all colors, with fishermen mending their nets. He and his sisters would swim. In the long evenings, he would join in the singing, accompanied by a guitar. Throughout his life, he was to remember these Basque songs.

On a hot day in August 1916, when Pedro was eight years old, tragedy befell the happy family. While the hot sun beat down on the streets of Bilbao, the blinds of No.7 Pelota Street were drawn. This was the last family reunion. In one bedroom, six candles burned round a bed where Pedro's beloved mother had died. His father led his four heart-broken daughters and his son Perico—for that was the affectionate name given to Pedro by his family—in prayer. His father put his arm round the sobbing boy. "Perico, your mother was a saint." Then pointing to the Virgin of Begonja, in a small chapel, he said: "From now on, she will be your mother." Pedro later recorded that he then understood "more than anything," that God's mother was his mother.

The five young children returned to the house of their aunt Magarita where they lived while their mother was ill. Then they came back to No. 7. The house was now empty; a well-loved mother was no longer there. This was a terrible gap for the young boy. His father tried to fill the gap. But he, too, had been devastated. He took refuge in his work, drawing plans for houses, submitting an entry in a competition for a tower building in Begonja. He did not win. That made him more depressed. He gave up architecture, resorting only to his business of buying and selling minerals and other products of the mines, and to the education of his children. It was some time before his father returned to singing with his magnificent tenor voice in the Jesuit College of Ordunja.

Pedro started school at Alameda Recalde. There were 25 to 30 pupils from the middle and upper classes, along with scholarship boys, in his class. One of them, Jose Isasi, remembers him as very happy, open, and excellent in his studies. Pedro was a normal boy. He was good at soccer and his voice would often be heard in the streets. He later jokingly attributed his long nose to an argument with a street lamp-post! He was not very pious but loved going to church.

As the only boy in the family, he was much loved by his sisters. "He was absolutely charming," says his sister Maria, who was four years older than he. She would help him with his homework. If he was stuck on a problem, he would shout, "Come on, Maria. Help!"

When eleven, he was initiated into the Congregation of Mary Immaculate, a sodality run by Fr. Angel Basterra, famous in Bilbao for his work with young children. In 1922, when he was fifteen, Pedro was on a committee of the sodality which had its own literary publication, Flowers and Fruits, where the young gave expression to their views. In the March 1923 issue, Pedro had a piece in which he made curious, prophetic allusions to Japan and the missionary Francs Xavier, saying that he would like to emulate what Francis had done.

After he finished his baccalaureate in Bilbao in 1922, Pedro applied to study medicine at the University of Madrid. When he was young, his mother used to say that Pedro would become a priest. Now his father said, "The priest has gone down another road. Pedro is going to be a priest of bodies."

The face of a young, handsome sixteen-year old, his hair perfectly brushed, his tie impeccably tied on his shirt, looked out of the window as the train from Bilbao chugged its way up the Cantabrian Mountains, across the Ebro River to Burgos, then along the flat plateau to Valladolid. His eyes enlarged as they stared at the stately buildings and tall church spires. Then across the Duero, up over the Sierra de Guadarrama, then down to the capital, Madrid. He had been admitted to the Medical Faculty of San Carlos at the University of Madrid. He stepped off the train carrying his suitcase. A station porter with a thick mustache and in large overalls offered help, but the young Pedro could manage. Everywhere beckoned the painted machines dispensing cigarettes and chocolates. A policeman with a grand air, somewhat overweight, surveyed the milling passengers. Pedro wondered if he could ever run fast enough to catch a miscreant. A young man, his hand behind her back, led a young girl forward. They both had the air and manners of the "twenties."

Pedro crossed the station forecourt and made for the house of his married sister, Margarita, lugging his suitcase. Old Ford cars, the ultimate of elegance, drove past, the chaperones of young ladies in the back seat. The avenues were so broad and clean, the streetlights so high. Music from pianolas, playing the 'pop' songs of the 20's, blared out from the sidewalk cafes. There was dancing at the Ritz but no 'tango'—that had been prohibited by the Archbishop.

Those were also difficult and dangerous times. There was much political unrest in the country. Social tensions, the class struggle, assassinations, all added fuel to the impending confrontation. It was dangerous to be a head of government. Dato, the Prime Minister had been gunned down by anarchist assassins from a sidecar in Independence Square in the heart of the capital. The idea of a coup was in the air. Finally, on the nights of September 12 and 13, 1923, a military dictatorship under General Miguel Primo de Rivera overthrew the civilian government. At the same time, another General—Francisco Franco—was getting married to a young girl, Carmen Polo. In the United States, a new President was inaugurated. In Russia, the first socialist constitution began. In Tokyo, then only a name to Pedro Arrupe, 100,000 people had perished in an earthquake.

For Pedro, the bustling life of a university student in a large metropolis was a huge emotional wrench from the safe and secure haven he had known in Bilbao. Pedro studied hard, spending many hours over his books. One day, he emerged from the splendid, old eighteen-century building of San Carlos and walked up the street to greet his friend Enrique Chacon. Enrique was studying mining engineering. Together, they walked along the Gran Via to Pi y Margail building where the Catholic students had a residence on the ninth floor, and where Enrique lived. They were a great bunch of students, lively, full of fun. Most of them came from Bilbao, with a few Catalans. At Christmas of that year, Pedro, too, took up his residence there.

The students, 25 of them, would cook for themselves. Occasionally, a mother of one of the students would assist in the cooking. It was a happy community, full of laughter and jokes. The medical students would dangle skeletons, borrowed from the anatomy classes, outside the windows of their neighbors below to frighten them until one day, an irate neighbor smashed in the head of the tormenting skeleton.

Pedro loved the opera—*The Barber of Seville*, *Aida*, and *Lohengrin*. As he later wrote:

> I liked the theatre, music, and opera—very much. Ah, the opera! We were the cheering section and we would go to buy the tickets at a bar where the plates were made of metal and the silverware was attached to the tables by little chains; you see the kind of place it was! We were young then.

> At that time, Miguel Fleta was making his debut. He had been a vegetable seller, leading his donkey through the streets of Zaragosa, and he used to shout out his wares enthusiastically. As an opera singer, he had a powerful voice, but not yet very well trained. In Madrid, he was a great success, and he was often interrupted by the enthusiasm of his admirers. He would beg the public on his knees to allow him to continue; and our group, we would applaud and cheer him even more.

One day, Pedro met Enrique on the ninth floor of the students' residence. He was pacing up and down the corridor, a sheaf of notes in his hand. He had had no sleep at all.

"What's the matter?" Pedro asked. It was examination time.

"My father is going to kill me if I don't pass," Enrique replied.

Pedro encouraged him. He let Enrique study in his own room to keep distraction away from him. Pedro would wake him with water on his head at 5 a.m. The concentrated effort worked and Enrique's father did not have to resort to murder!

Pedro himself was a good student. In his first year (1922), he won the First Prize for Anatomical studies. In his second year, he won the Physiology Prize. In 1926, he won the prize for Therapeutics.

Pedro went home to Bilbao for his holidays. On one of these holidays, Pedro met a Columbian, Juan Jaramillo, who was doing his theological studies in Valkenburg in Holland, and had come to the Basque country on vacation. He was about to be ordained a Jesuit priest. As an ordination present, Juan asked his parents, who were coming from Columbia in South America, if, on their way through Europe, they could invite Pedro to accompany them to be present at his ordination and first Mass. The parents bought a car in Spain and took Pedro along with them through Europe. They had their young daughter Marie with them. No doubt, in the course of the journey, they came to consider Pedro as a most suitable son-in-law. But Marie later married a renowned Colombian doctor. The son of the union was later, like his uncle Juan, to enter the Society of Jesus.

---

Pedro and his friend Enrique joined the Society of St. Vincent de Paul, an organization that provided aid to the poor and destitute. On their visits to the poor of Madrid, they entered a totally new world, unknown to them, in the poorer districts of the city. There, pain and misery and hunger and abandonment thrived; there, widows begged for bread for their hungry half-naked children; there, the sick begged for charity.

One day, they entered a dwelling—it couldn't be called a house—of a poor family. It was 4 o'clock in the afternoon.

"What are you eating? Pedro asked the urchin in rags.

"A roll," he replied. "I suppose you have a roll at breakfast time. For me, this is my first food. We only eat once a day."

"Does your father work?" Enrique joined in, shattered by seeing such poverty and misery, first hand.

"No, he doesn't—because I have no father."

Like a starving dog, the urchin would prowl through the streets, collecting bread—dried bread, dirty bread to take back to his widowed mother and his younger brothers and sisters.

Pedro and Enrique had been directed to visit a destitute widow named Luisa in the district of Vallecas. They asked a doubled-up woman who was sweeping her doorstep if she knew where Luisa lived. With difficulty the old lady straightened up, holding firmly on her broom handle. Speaking through the large gaps in her teeth, she replied, "Luisa? Yes, she lives in No. 10," she said pointing. "Up the stairs, in room 10. Two widows live there." She leaned on her broomstick. "Are you two from the Vincent de Paul Society? I've seen you around." Then giving a whistle through her broken teeth, the eighty-year-old sighed, "Jesus! What handsome young boys!"

The two smiled and headed for No. 10. In the doorway, they met a boy, a young lad already with a 'doctorate in street-survival.'

"It's this way, sir, to #10. Mind the holes in the stairs or you'll end up in the basement."

The whole place was dark, dirty, disgusting. There was poverty in abundance here. They gave the boy some candy they had brought from the cake shop for his assistance. They stood opposite the small door to No. 10. Deafening shouting emerged from the other side of the door. A woman's voice somehow managed to make itself heard above the din.

"Sounds like a madhouse," said Enrique. "I think we'd be safer with lions in a cage."

Pedro knocked on the door.

"Who's that?" a woman's voice screamed.

Pedro knocked again.

"Who's that?" again she screamed. "Come on, man, speak up. Who is it?"

Slowly Pedro creaked open the door. What a sight! It was beyond their comprehension. They had never experienced anything like this.

Two women stood in the room and six dirty, unkempt, ill-clothed children with sunken sallow cheeks, stared at them out of frightened eyes behind their mothers' skirts where they had taken refuge like terrified chicks.

"You're not from here?" one of the women asked.

"No. We're from the 'S.V.P'."

That answer brought relief to the women. Mistrust disappeared. The ice thawed completely when the hungry children were given sweets. The room was sparsely furnished—a lop-sided table, a bed with a soiled mattress, a cupboard, some broken chairs.

"Well, what do you think of my palace?" Luisa asked.

"Do you all live here? Enrique asked, disbelief in his voice.

"We all live, and play together in this room."

"But where do you sleep?"

"Let's show them," the other woman replied.

As if at a signal, all six boys leapt onto the bed, on top of the blanket, three against the headboard, three against the foot of the bed.

"And in the space between them, we rest. We don't sleep because the children fall on top of us," the woman explained.

The two women had little or no money. While one went out to earn something, the other stayed behind to look after the children. In the morning, they had garlic soup and bread. It was cold; the children stayed in bed, as they had no jerseys. Pedro and Enrique gave the two women what money they had, and the rest of sweets to the children.

They stepped gingerly down the rotten staircase, avoiding the easy descent to the ground floor, which was clearly visible through the gaping holes in the wood. They walked for a long while without speaking. They were too overcome at seeing such poverty. They passed the cake shop where normally they would have bought some cakes. Not today! They had given away all their money. Besides, it would have been immoral to buy cakes in the midst of such hunger and squalor and misery.

———————————

There was the usual chatter of voices as the young men sat on the wooden benches that rose higher and higher looking down on the lecturer's desk. Before them they had their notepads, and into their hands their pens or pencils. Suddenly the chattering ceased. You could hear a suture needle drop in the lecture room. A middle-aged man with a wide broad face, dapper, a small tie under his chin walked briskly into the room. He looked at the clean blackboard, then made for the lectern. Over his little round glasses he peered at the students.

"Good morning!" Professor Juan Negrin said.

"Good morning, sir," the students chorused.

"You will remember," the Professor of Physiology began, and then stopped. He started again. "*Some of you* will remember!"

The students laughed.

"Yes, some of you will remember," ... a smile on his face to acknowledge his joke at their expense. "We were discussing Vesalius."

Professor Negrin suddenly stopped again. He looked to his left, up the rows of eager faces, then to his right, above the bright young faces.

Where's Arrupe?" he asked.

The faces looked at each other.

"I don't see Arrupe today?"

That was odd. No professor ever inquired about the absence of any of his students. Valentin Matila and Enrique Poyuelo, who were later to become eminent physicians, frowned at each other. Why should someone as blatantly atheistic as the Professor worry about the presence or the absence of someone who stood out from the class of atheists, agnostics and unbelievers, by being a practicing Christian.

A young man put up his hand. The Professor lifted his chin towards the student.

"I think he's gone home to Bilbao."

The young man who put up his hand was Severo Ochoa, who in 1959, thirty-three years later was awarded the Nobel Prize for Medicine for his synthesis of RNA (ribonucleic acid) which with DNA (deoxyribonucleic acid) is a vital constituent of the living cell.

Arrupe had, indeed, returned home to Bilbao. His father was dying. Through his tears, he could see a desolate scene—his sisters gathered round the bed of their father, Don Marcellino, choking between life and death. Outside the window, he could see an altar being prepared, covered with a carpet of flowers in readiness for the procession of the Sacred Heart. He could remember himself as a young boy shielding a small burning candle in his hand, following behind his enormous father through the streets of Bilbao.

He later wrote: "I looked out of the window. I could see Fr. Basterra coming to the doorway. I rushed down the stairs to meet him."

"'How is Don Marcellino?'"

"'Bad,' I replied. 'He has already lost consciousness.'"

"'Poor Perico!' Fr. Basterra replied. 'How God is testing you!'"

"Poor Perico," indeed. His beloved father had taken his last breath. Aged nineteen, with a brilliant career before him, Pedro's world had collapsed about him. Margarita, Catalina, Maria, and Isabel, watched him sobbing; they hugged him, now the only support of the family. He wandered through the empty rooms; the photographs, the old smiles that would never return to life. He remembered Fr. Basterra pointing to a statue of the Sacred Heart on the altar. "This is your real father who died for you!" "Since then," wrote Arrupe, many years later, "Jesus has been my real Father."

# 3 From Doctor to Priest

D AY BY DAY, the interrogation in the Yamaguchi prison continued relentlessly. Pedro Arrupe remained in solitary confinement. There was no letting up in the hard discipline and
regime of prison life. Prisoners were never allowed out of the building,
except when they were taken to the baths down the street.

As Arrupe was being led down the street in his filthy clothes, dirty,
unshaven, he heard a voice shout: "There's Professor Arrupe. Look!
There!"

He looked across the road where a group of University students was
returning from their lessons. Arrupe taught classes in Spanish at the
University. One or two of the students laughed, but most were silent,
visibly shocked at seeing their teacher, whom they liked, being
marched along like a common felon.

"I wonder what crime he has committed?" they wondered.

He felt, as Christ must have felt, led like an animal, to face the
Roman tribunal.

One day, Arrupe asked the guard if he could shave. The guard didn't
know what Arrupe was talking about. That was understandable since
the Japanese grow no hair on their chins. Arrupe tried to explain, moving
his right hand round his cheeks to mimic pre-shave lathering. The guard
finally asked the foreigner to put his request in writing, which Arrupe
did. The next day, at 7 o'clock, two soldiers brought in a large bowl of
boiling water. He could shave. All the soldiers turned up to watch the
strange performance, which they had never witnessed before.

Another day, Arrupe heard his guards arguing whether it was water
or the cloud that came first.

"Let's ask the foreigner."

They filed into his cell.

Arrupe took the occasion to talk of things cosmic—and also about
the existence of God. The soldiers listened attentively. In fact, this
conversation resulted in a sort of daily catechism class. Trying to get

through to his audience made Arrupe further realize the difference between the two cultures. But a friendship developed between the prisoner and the guards. Indeed, one day, the chief guard came to Arrupe asking him for his advice on whether he should marry a girl he had not yet seen!

Day after day, night after night, Arrupe was held in solitary confinement. His back became more painful from sleeping with only a *tatami* (mat) separating him from the hard stone floor, cold and damp. The monotonous diet, too, was taking its toll on him. He would have preferred bread and water to the fibrous turnip and concentrated *sampi* which made him wretch. On other days, it would be *zosui*, a simple stew of rice and vegetables. Sometimes it would be a bowl of unwashed rice with a small salted sprat. He prayed a lot, of course. But after days and nights of solitary confinement, it was sometimes difficult, as Job found in his leprosy, to raise one's voice in praise of God.

One morning, he pricked up his ears as footsteps approached. The cell gate clanged open. Arrupe was led out for another round of questioning. He shielded his eyes from the light. He stood before a table in the center of which sat a bespectacled officer with a long face and a goatee beard. On the major's right sat another officer. Soon the two were joined by another, who limped in, using a walking stick as a crutch. He wore battle ribbons on his chest. He had been wounded in the many wars Japan had fought in China and Manchuria.

The major opened the questioning.

"There seems to be some discrepancy in your evidence. You say you are a priest?"

Fr. Arrupe nodded.

"This letter," the interrogating officer said, holding up one of Arrupe's letters that had been confiscated during the search of his premises, "shows you were at Vienna at a medical conference."

Arrupe nodded again.

"So are you a doctor or a priest?"

"I am both," Arrupe replied.

The officer frowned.

Arrupe explained further: "Before becoming a priest, I studied medicine."

"You mean you gave up the profession of a doctor to become a priest?"

Arrupe nodded yet again.

This was a time when the Buddhist faith, any religion, in fact, was not strong in Japan. The interrogator could not understand why anyone would give up a prestigious, lucrative profession, like medicine, to work in poverty for some invisible God.

"Why would anyone do that?" he asked.

"I changed because of certain happenings in Lourdes."

"Lourdes? What is that?"

"In the southwest of France, in 1858, the virgin Mary appeared on eighteen occasions to a fourteen-year-old peasant girl named Bernadette Soubirous. Since then, miraculous cures have taken place there."

"Miraculous? You mean you believe in miracles? A man of science believing in miracles?!"

"I believe them because I saw them. I was present."

"That's fantastic. Tell us more."

"It's a long story," Fr. Arrupe warned.

"Don't worry. We have all the time in the world to listen to such fantasies."

"The first miracle occurred in 1926. I had gone to Lourdes during my last year at the Faculty of Medicine in Madrid. I was with my sisters. My father had just died. It was in the hope of taking our minds off the grief."

Arrupe related the events and the effect they had on him. In July of that year (1926), the train from Bilbao rattled along to France. There were good views of the sea. At Irun, they crossed the border. More beautiful views of the sea arose as the train passed Hendaye, then past Blarritz, to Bayonne, Pau. The Pyrenees, brilliant-green, rose higher and higher in the background. The sisters trembled with excitement as the tall towers of the Basilica of Lourdes came into view. The river Gave bubbled along beside the train tracks. Arrupe had a premonition, undefinable, that this was going to be a memorable visit.

The train chugged to a stop. The passengers alighted. The station was crowded. *Brancardiers*, wearing their *bretelles* (leather shoulder straps), helped unload the stretchers off the train. Boy scouts and young girls in uniform helped with the sick. The five family members shuffled in and out of the throng of pilgrims. They crossed the train tracks and emerged in the bright sun. It was hot, but the air was fresh and inviting. They passed down the street with the shops all selling the same goods— souvenirs—holy pictures, rosaries, bottles of "Lourdes water."

Pedro went to the Medical Verification Bureau, to offer his services as a doctor in the examination of cases and to verify any so-called "miraculous" cures that were reported, on some rare occasions.

So often he had heard his professors and students at the faculty of San Carlos scoff at the "superstitions" surrounding Lourdes and the so-called "miracle cures." Well, now was his chance to investigate and verify them first-hand.

That next day, the family of four sisters and their brother, now the head of the family since their father's death, made for the *Domain* leading to the Basilica. The crowds were huge. They squeezed in through the tall iron gates. In the distance rose the magnificent wide steps leading up to the Basilica. *Brancardiers*, pushing invalid carriages, dodged the people as best they could. An official put a finger to his mouth, admonishing the crowds to be 'silent'. They turned right to the *Gave*, bubbling past.

Apart from the shuffling of feet, all was quiet. To the left of them were the taps from which devout pilgrims were filling their leather bottles. Then they came to the Shrine of Our Lady of Lourdes, built into the grotto where in 1858, a white Lady is alleged to have appeared 18 times to a young fourteen-year–old shepherdess. The statue was sur-rounded by hundreds of burning candles. From the roof of the grotto hung hundreds of crutches of those who no longer needed them.

Most of the time, all was quiet or as quiet as several thousand praying pilgrims could be. But that day, the silence was to be broken by a thunderous ovation.

The doors of the Basilica opened and the usual large procession began. Under a canopy covered in color-of-gold and carried by bemedaled chief *brancardiers*, the bishop dressed in heavy vestments, carried the Blessed Sacrament in a gold monstrance. The procession wound its way between the hundreds of sick pilgrims lying out on their stretchers or sitting up in their invalid carriages, *brancardiers* and nurses tending each of the sick. Every ten yards or so, the procession would slow, the bishop would raise the Blessed Sacrament and bless the sick in front of him, making the sign of the cross. Between the murmur of the rosaries, a priest's voice, quivering with loud emotion shouted in a voice, "Our Lady of Lourdes, take pity on me! Our Lady of Lourdes, take pity on me!" The people choked; the tears flowed abundantly.

A nun wincing with pain with every movement, her spine in a plaster jacket, yet always uncomplaining, looked up at the white host. She had Pott's disease, tuberculosis of the spine. The x-rays showed the disease was eating away her vertebrae. Though words came out from her only with difficulty, she had begged to be allowed a blessing at the Blessed Sacrament procession.

Then something happened. The bishop, aghast, lowered the monstrance; the canopy-bearers moved and upset its neat rectangular shape; a *brancardier* rushed forward, followed by another, to hold the body down.

The paralyzed nun rose from her stretcher, shouted "I'm cured!" and extended her arm toward the Eucharist, and then fell on her knees before it. The loudspeaker picked up her shout of "I'm cured." The next instant, the crowd burst into a thunderous ovation of 'Miracle.' You could have heard the noise in Massabielle. Bedlam ensued as the realization of what had happened hit the stunned crowd. The *brancardiers* immediately formed a strong phalanx with their *bretelles* to keep the crowds from rushing to touch the cured nun.

Later, Arrupe as an authorized doctor of the Verification Bureau was able to examine the nun, and the x-ray photographs of her condition. Arrupe later described the event: "In one solemn moment, the paralyzed nun and Jesus Christ came face to face. I don't know how they looked at each other. But in that instant, there was a great contact of love between them."

A few days later, Arrupe was present to witness another miracle-cure. Lying on a stretcher, along with hundreds of other sick pilgrims, was a seventy-five-year old lady who had traveled across France from Brussels. She had advanced cancer of the stomach. When the surgeons opened her up, they realized the hopelessness of her situation. They felt they had to tell her how near she was to dying.

"Is there nothing you can do?" she implored.

"Only a miracle can cure you," they replied.

The old lady composed herself and then, with a faith that confounded the people around her, said, "So why don't we prepare ourselves for a miracle?"

The doctors assumed she had lost her mind with death approaching.

"If I go to Lourdes, I can be cured," she said in a soft voice.

"In your condition, it would be impossible for you to make the trip to Lourdes. You would merely hasten your death."

"What's the difference if I die in one week in route to France or if I die here in one month? I prefer to risk a cure. If I get to Lourdes, I am sure the Virgin will cure me."

She watched the procession of the Blessed Sacrament go past. How she prayed! But there was no change in her condition. She had the faith that can move mountains. She asked to be taken to the Baths where she could be immersed in the water. Again, nothing unusual! But when she got back to the Hospice, she said she was hungry—for the first time in years. She ate some solid food without any problems of digestion. Her appetite increased; she ate more solid food. In three days, she was walking around Lourdes in perfect health. Arrupe was there when the verifying doctors, many of whom were unbelievers or agnostics, x-rayed her stomach. There was no trace of the cancer that had been plainly visible before.

On another day, there were at least 12,000 pilgrims jam-packed in the square before the Basilica. The huge number of pilgrims had attracted Arrupe and his sisters, who were then sucked up in the slow-moving mass of people.

"Look at that poor boy—there in his invalid carriage," one of Pedro's sisters said, pointing as she did so. He was a lad of about twenty years.

His face bore the appearance of one suffering from paralysis. He was being wheeled along by a nurse in uniform; his suffering mother, with a sad face, followed behind. Goodness knows for how many years she had prayed for a miracle.

As the Blessed Sacrament was carried in front of the paralyzed young man, he got up from his chair and shouted that he was cured. Immediately, the huge crowd took up the cry, "Miracle! Miracle!" The *brancardiers* rushed to the boy's protection to prevent him from being crushed to death. Before the violent emotion of the throng could reach him, they had formed a human barrier around him with their *bretelles*. Again, with his medical permit, Arrupe was able to investigate the young man's case at close hand and to certify if there could be no possible natural explanation for what had happened.

———————————————

There was a pause. Arrupe was tired, not only from talking but from standing for so long before the officers.

The Major broke the silence. "So we had better start believing in miracles," he said with a laugh turning to his companions who shared the little joke. 'What about you, lieutenant? We could send you to Lourdes for a cure!" the Major laughed out raucously; the crippled lieutenant merely smiled at this crude joke at his expense.

Some tea was brought in for the officers. There was none for Arrupe.

"Then what happened?" the Major asked.

Arrupe continued with the events of his life.

Pedro and his sisters returned to Bilbao.

The sisters commented that their brother seemed lost in thought as he gazed out on the green fields and the tall Pyrenees beyond. It seemed as though something of his heart had remained behind in the Shrine with its incredible silence beside the murmuring Gave. The same God who had spoken to him through those poor people living in that filthy, overcrowded hovel in Vallecas, was speaking to him again through the miracles among the incurable. It was as if Jesus Himself, the friend of the poor and outcasts, was walking past and calling him to Himself, to imitate Him in His poverty and charity towards those unfortunates of the world rejected by society. He was beginning to hear the cry of those shipwrecked in this life.

Pedro returned to Madrid to begin his post-graduate medical studies. Everything in Madrid was the same. The same porter swept the streets; the same man with the thick moustache would read his paper at the same table in the bar while drinking his coffee. But Pedro was not the same. After the death of his father, Pedro felt like an orphan, without any roots. He felt imprisoned in a dark black hole. In him, a decision was slowly maturing. Everyone noticed the change.

"What's the matter, Perico?" everyone asked.

"Oh! My problems! I told you about Lourdes. I'm thinking about what to do with my life. And what about you—when are you getting married?" "I'm not sure, either," his friend Enrique replied.

Pedro ran his fingers across the textbooks tucked neatly into the shelf. He pulled out two at random—a textbook of anatomy, another of physiology. Inexplicably, they slipped through his fingers and fell on the floor. Was this a premonition? He asked himself: "What am I doing here? A few years of life—and then?" The destitute he had met in that room in Vallecas had removed the blinds from his eyes. There was another route, another way. He made up his mind. Instead of devoting his life to curing the ills of the body, he would devote his life to curing the ills of the soul. As he later recorded: "The misery and sadness in the world which needs consoling found in me a vocation much more sublime, which up till now had only been a dream."

When the word got round, his colleagues in the Faculty of Medicine thought him mad. Though they came from different backgrounds and from all parts of the country; one common characteristic that bound together most of the students—and the professors—was that they were atheists or unbelievers, supporting the popular social principles of Marxism and communism.

When Arrupe announced he was going to spend a vacation at the Office of Verification in the Medical Center at the grotto of Lourdes, they had scoffed at him.

"Don't be stupid, Pedro. You can't believe all that rubbish. It's all superstition. Miracles!"

One of them said, "The only miracle I hope for is that I pass my exams!"

Two young doctors were passing the door of the Faculty Boardroom. There was unusual noise emerging from that hallowed sanctuary.

"I will not sign. I refuse to."

They recognized the voice of Professor Negrin, the Dean of the Faculty.

"But you have to, Professor," another exclaimed in a loud voice. "He was chosen unanimously by all of us—including you," the voice went on.

"I will not sign."

"Are you refusing to sign because he is becoming a priest, a Jesuit?"

There was no reply from Negrin.

"That would be most unjust. That would be clear discrimination."

"If the students hear about this," another Professor remarked, "there will be a riot."

The students did hear about it. Although there was no riot, they were highly indignant that the student who had been voted as the best student of the final year of medical studies should be denied the First Prize of 500 pesetas—now a small sum, but then quite a significant amount. That student was Pedro Arrupe. Don Marcellino Oreja, President of the Students Union, organized a collection among themselves and decided to award 2,000 pesetas—a very large sum then— to Arrupe. For Arrupe, the prize money didn't matter. He was soon to be taking a vow of poverty anyway.

---

The afternoon after he had given this account of his transition from medicine to the Jesuit priesthood, a *sochu* appeared at his prison cell to question him. Since the cell was bare, a table and chair, along with pen and paper, were brought in. He was asked his name and that of his father and brothers and wife. To the surprise of Arrupe, he then picked up his papers and left. Arrupe had expected a long interrogation.

Two days later, the same short interrogation occurred. As the interpreter was leaving, Arrupe asked him why he was being held in prison. The *sochu* stopped: "Do you really want to hear the charges against you?"

"Yes," Arrupe replied.

The policeman took out about one hundred letters from his brief-case. For the next forty-five minutes, the policeman, sitting at the table, read continuously the charges made against him, a mixture of political and religious accusations. The man explained this was a list of his activities before the war. In effect, it was a summary embellished with imagination of what the first interrogator had taken in his interviews with Arrupe.

Fr. Arrupe turned to the *sochu*. "I know I have a lot of defects. But am I really as bad as that?" he asked, a quizzical smile on his face, tilted in characteristic poise.

All the charges against Arrupe were lies, but how could he prove they were? Despite his innate optimism, his future began to look bleak. Arrupe confessed that he became frightened. His lack of sleep and poor diet had eroded his nervous system. He had become weaker and weaker. Ghosts began to cross his imagination. For espionage, there would be only one punishment—death. The disturbing scenarios became more lurid—execution by firing squad or hanging or decapitation. Because he was a priest, they might conjure up some other, more barbaric form of execution—like those used in earlier times of persecution of the Christians. Like—burning at the stake, or the immersion in the boiling sulfurous water of the bubbling lakes at Mount Unzen, or the water torture—when huge amounts of water are poured into the body through the nose and mouth. Or another water punishment—tied to a stake at the water's edge so that when the tide came in the water would reach up to the chin and then recede and after some days, you would die of physical or mental exhaustion.

Or, perhaps, worst of all—the *ana-tsurushi*, hanging upside down in a pit of excrement. This was the most common method used to make the Christian convert apostatize. A *fumi-e*, an image or picture of the Virgin and Child, would be placed on the ground before the prisoners and they would be asked to trample on the picture. Or they would be called on to spit on the crucifix and declare the Blessed Virgin a whore, and if they refused, they would be subjected to the *ana-tsurushi*.

The victim was tightly bound around the body as high as the breast (one hand let free to give the signal of recantation) and then hung downwards from a gallows into a pit which usually contained excreta and other filth, the top of the pit being level with the victim's knees. Little incisions were made behind the ears so that one would not die immediately. The blood trickled out slowly, drop by drop, through the incisions and through the nose and mouth. [The stronger martyrs lived for more than a week in this position; the weaker did not survive more than a day or two.]

Would he ever apostatize? Never! Yet that is what Fr. Christopher Ferreira, S.J., had said. He had been in Japan as a missionary and Provincial, an inspiration to priests and people alike. At the height of the religious persecution, he had made his way into the Kamigata region to continue his apostolic work as an underground priest. He was finally caught. He was cross-examined by the magistrate Inoue, the Lord of Chikugo. He was sentenced to death in the pit. After six hours of agony, he finally cracked. He signaled with his free hand that he would apostatize. When a *fumi-e* was brought before him, he put his foot on the face of Christ. For nineteen years, he was allowed to live as a *Bonze* (Buddhist priest). But like Peter's denial at the cock-crow, this tale too had a happy heroic ending. Fr. Ferreira recanted and repaired the nineteen years of apostasy by dying in the same pit in Nagasaki, which had previously conquered him.

During these long hours of solitary confinement, despite such nightmares, Fr. Arrupe, he would later say, learned wisdom and inner dialogue "with the guest of my soul." Years later, when in Rome, ill with thrombosis, he confessed that this was the most instructive period of his life. "It was beautiful—the solitude with Christ, a mystical experience, nothing in my cell, only me and Christ." And his eyes filled with tears.

Christmas eve! He had been in prison nearly three weeks. That night while the city of Yamaguchi slept, he sat up, in silence, sorrowful. He imagined the Midnight Mass he would not be celebrating. It was unbearable.

He later described what followed:

> Instead of Christmas, it seemed to me more like Good Friday. My Christmas was being changed into the Passion and the blessed night into a sad Gethsemane. But then I heard a strange sound near one of the windows. It was the soft murmur of many voices which with muted accents sought to escape detection. I began to listen. If any of you have been in prison waiting for a sentence, you would appreciate the anxiety with which I followed those sounds which were now of themselves becoming an immediate source of suspicion. Such are the fears one feels within the four walls where one is detained.

> Suddenly above the murmur that was reaching me, there arose a soft sweet consoling Christmas carol, one of the songs I had myself taught my Christians. I was unable to contain myself. I burst into tears. They were my Christians who, heedless of the danger of being themselves imprisoned, had come to console me, their *Shimpu Sama* (their priest) who was away that Christmas night which hitherto we had always celebrated with such great joy!

After a few minutes, the carol of his parishioners died away into the silence and darkness of the city. He took courage. His crude cell became a Bethlehem.

Meanwhile, outside the jail, the Jesuits in Hiroshima were not inactive on Arrupe's behalf. Fr. LaSalle, the Superior, made contact with Professor Chabatta, Professor of Chemistry, who also held a high military rank. Could he intervene? The Professor came to *Yamaguchi* and spoke to Fr. Arrupe's captors. But they would not let him see Arrupe. He spoke to the jailers and this might have prompted less harsh treatment from his captors.

The interrogation continued. Arrupe was asked extensively about his entrance into the Jesuits and about his training as a member of their group. Back in his cell, he asked for a Japanese dictionary and some old magazines so that he might improve his knowledge of the Japanese language.

Brought again before his interrogators, he spoke about the difficulty of breaking the news of his decision to enter the Jesuits to his sisters. He waited until after Christmas, and then early in January of 1927, he let his sisters know. They were dumbfounded! "Perico, what about your career?!"

A few days later, he gave them a final hug, and together with his brother-in-law Sautu, journeyed to Loyola, the site of the Jesuit Novitiate. There, he discovered that besides his birth-certificate and other papers, he needed a letter of approval from his local bishop. Arrupe waited in a hotel in Loyola and in two weeks the letter arrived and he could begin his training.

The mentor for new Jesuit entrants is called "the Master of Novices." Arrupe's mentor during this period of his training was a tall, lean Basque with greying hair and ruddy cheeks named Fr. Garmendia. He and Pedro got along very well.

As part of these two years of initial training, Jesuits would spend one month in solitary prayer, making the Spiritual Exercises developed by St. Ignatius Loyola. They also were required in Arrupe's day, to spend a month learning how to cook, another working in hospitals and infirmaries, and another making a pilgrimage. On this pilgrimage, they were given neither food nor money, but had to beg their way en route, sleeping sometimes in the straw with cattle. The other months were spent studying the Constitutions of the Jesuit order written by St. Ignatius, learning how to pray, and living in community with the other new Jesuits.

Pedro was quite popular with the other Jesuit novices. Athletic, well-built, with angular features and a pointed nose, he had a wonderful sense of humor and could do marvelously funny imitations of other humans and animals. He was often fun to be with. He also had a great baritone singing voice.

During his first year of Novitiate, he had two surprising visits. One day, Enrique Chaldon, his very close friend from his days in Madrid, appeared and told "Perico" that he too had decided to leave his studies [he had been preparing to become an engineer], end his serious friendship with a young woman, and enter the Jesuit order.

The other surprising visitor was his former Dean at the School of Medicine, Professor Negrin, who, infuriated at Pedro's decision to leave medicine for the Jesuit order, had refused to allow him to receive the prize for first place accomplishments in his medical class. Negrin had come to tell Arrupe his reason for his refusal: "I was trying to motivate you to return to medicine where I think you could have a great career. I like you a lot!" Arrupe did not change his decision, but the future General of the Jesuit Order and the future Prime Minister of the Socialist Republic of Spain hugged each other before Professor Negrin left. Pedro continued in his Jesuit calling.

In November, 1928, near the end of Pedro's novice training, the Novice Master, Fr. Garmendia developed cancer of the stomach and on December 20, he died in Arrupe's arms.

The following year, Pedro took his first vows of chastity, poverty, and obedience, and moved on in his course of Jesuit training to study the Classics and Humanities, with special emphasis on the Greek tragedians—Sophocles and Euripides.

It was during this period, in the eight day retreat which Jesuits make each year, Arrupe was moved to ask to go to Japan as a missionary. The response to his written request was simply an acknowledgement, with neither negation nor affirmation. He was told to continue in his studies. His Dean, at the time, Fr. Ibero, said to him prophetically, "Perico, don't worry! You will get to Japan." For the next ten years, Fr. Ibero's words echoed through his soul.

The 1930's began, and Arrupe and his class moved onto the very old Monastery of San Salvador de Onya, a former Benedictine monastery now used as the main seminary college of the Society of Jesus, where 300 young Jesuits pursued their study of philosophy and theology. Here he began his study of philosophy, which for him would require two years rather than the usual three, because of his prior studies at the School of Medicine in Madrid.

But the stay there would be very short. On April 14, 1931, a Socialist Spanish Republic was proclaimed, and in June, it was promulgated that "Spain has ceased being Catholic" and that "the Society of Jesus was to be dissolved and all of its assets nationalized." The Jesuits were given a few days to leave the country.

On February 13, 1932, Arrupe with 300 Spanish Jesuits traveled by train to Marneffe in Belgium. Their lives there would be quite spartan.

After two years of study of philosophy, Pedro was sent to Valkenburg in Holland to study theology, majoring especially in moral theology, under the aegis of the well-known moral theologian, Fr. Huerth.

There, one day to his surprise, he received a letter for the President of the Association of Saints Cosmas and Damian informing him that he had been selected to give two papers at the International Congress of Eugenics, in Vienna. This was a topic of immense interest at the time, an interest prompted by the Nazi Party's blueprint to produce "a master Nordic race" by selective breeding and by the elimination of lesser races and people. Adolph Hitler's brain-child!

Arrupe's presentation there, made before some of the greatest minds of that era—Niedemeyer, Germelli, Balbot, Allers, Carp—was a stalwart declaration of the Catholic Church's reservations on such questions as "selective breeding," "castration," and "sterilization." To Pedro's surprise, his presentation was greeted with thunderous applause.

Arrupe continued his studies in theology, and on July 30, 1936, he and forty of his Jesuit brothers were ordained to the priesthood. Unfortunately, because a civil war had just broken out in Spain, none of the seminarians' loved ones could be present for their ordination in Valkenburg.

Two months after his ordination, Fr. Arrupe received a telegram telling him to prepare to travel to the United States. It had been decided to have him specialize in moral theology. For several summer months, he would have special training in psychiatry and clinical psychology at the Catholic University of America in Washington, D.C., under the guidance of the celebrated Carthusian scholar, Fr. Moore, drawing inspiration from the profound writings of Fr. Agostino Gemelli. He would then move on to St. Mary's College in Kansas for his final year of theology, 1936–37, followed by a final year of spiritual formation in Cleveland, Ohio.

In June of 1938, through the intervention of Fr. McMenamy, the Jesuit who had directed Pedro during his final year of spiritual formation and who had been sent to Rome for an important meeting there, Fr. Arrupe received a letter from the Jesuit General, missioning him to go to Japan. He would sail in two months. He was overjoyed!

But in the meanwhile, he offered his pastoral services to imprisoned Hispanics at a maximum security prison in New York State. There were more than 500 Hispanics there with no priest to look after their pastoral care. Arrupe volunteered.

Most likely, he did not detail to his Japanese interrogators those events which later led him to say: "Had it not been for my dream of working in Japan, I would have remained with the outcast Hispanics for the rest of my life. My work with these men moved me deeply."

His first encounter was with a prisoner who, in the words of one of his guards, "had done everything. He is the worst!" Pedro was able to touch the man's heart and to bring him assurance of God's forgiveness and of God's love. At the end of their conversation, in the man's cell, they shook hands.

Somewhat later, going into "Death Row" where men awaited execution, Fr. Arrupe talked with a Panamanian prisoner slated for execution. They talked of the man's life, of his deep love and concern for his son and his daughter, both still in Panama. The man spoke of the "child-abusive" character of the two wives, whom he had killed. Arrupe was able to arrange for his two children to be put into the care of a group of nuns living in the man's hometown in Panama. He also was able to give the man absolution before he was led away to execution and to offer him the assurance Jesus had given to the penitent thief: "This day, you shall be with me in Paradise."

Shortly before he finished his two months service in this prison, Arrupe went to say "Goodbye" to "his friends." The Hispanic prisoners were then out in the prison yard. One of them said to Arrupe: "We are going to give you a farewell present." Suddenly, 700 voices sang

Latino-American songs in Spanish accompanied by home-made musical instruments. Arrupe was overwhelmed!

When the nostalgic serenade ended, there was total silence in the baseball field. The prisoners were expecting a word from "their priest." Arrupe thanked them, and then in his splendid baritone voice sang a Basque *Zortziko* (dance ballad), full of tenderness.

As he narrated this story of his years in the Jesuit order leading up to his arrival in Japan, Arrupe was still in solitary confinement. The interrogation continued. At midnight on January 11, 1942, he was asleep in his cell. Suddenly, the cell door was thrown open. In the doorway stood officials, carrying under their arms papers and documents. One man was dressed in what seemed like Buddhist garb. Arrupe wondered if he, like the Jesuit martyrs of Japan, was to be asked to convert to Buddhism or be killed. He was led out of his cell to where the officials had seated themselves at a table. The man dressed like a monk, who looked anything but a *Kempeitai* police chief, led the interrogation. Arrupe was questioned for the next 14 hours. They wanted to know everything about his private life, the time he woke up, the time he went to bed, the time he prayed, the time he meditated.

The grilling went on for another 23 hours without stop. He was asked about his beliefs. Arrupe spoke of his commitment to the two great commandments—love of God and love of neighbor. He was then asked if he believed that the Emperor Tenno Heika "is God, the Creator of the World." Knowing that this was the Japanese faith, Arrupe, nonetheless, replied "No."

Arrupe was next questioned about politics.

Finally, the interrogator dressed in monk's robes read back to Fr. Arrupe all he had said in the 37 hour exchange. He was pleased that what was read back to him was quite exact.

He was asked then to put his fingerprints at the bottom of the document to signify he agreed with it. Pedro was happy to oblige.

Just as he was leaving, the interrogator called him back. "What is this 'Jesuit' you talked about?" Arrupe replied, "Jesuits are a group founded to go where needs are greatest and where there are no others to help with those needs. They come for those persons who are either totally neglected or inadequately attended, those on the margins of society, those who have been denied their dignity, those who are voiceless and powerless. They often give their lives for this cause."

The interrogator dressed in monk's robes raised his eyebrows: "Such people exist?" Arrupe nodded: "Yes, there are about 30,000 in the world."

Arrupe was the allowed back to his cell after a day and an half of continuous interrogation. But he didn't get much rest. Half an hour later, he was called to the prison Governor's office.

"You are free," the Governor said. "You may leave the prison when you like." Arrupe was stunned. A few hours earlier, he was expecting execution. Now he was free! His head reeled.

The Governor explained why he had been detained. "The information we received from the Kempeitai on your activities were very negative. That was why it was necessary to search your house and detain you. We kept you in prison to analyze you. In cases like yours, the best way of judging the innocence or guilt of the accused is to examine the person closely in his everyday activities. We Japanese can intuit from the exterior mannerisms and behavior what the inner man is like. Just as a picture can give a glimpse of the character of the painter, one's exterior manner reveals one's inner being."

Thus, it was that Arrupe's internal completeness, his simplicity, his transparency of soul convinced the police of his innocence and personal integrity. As the commander told him, "You submitted to every suffering we imposed on you. You never complained about anything. You remained dedicated to your prayer and your studies."

Arrupe got up to thank the Governor.

"Thank Me?" the Governor asked in surprise. "Why should you thank me? We have been cruel to you! Maybe, that was the stress of the war."

"I am not resentful toward you. You are someone who has done me good."

"Done you good? ... Me?"

"Yes. You have taught me to suffer. I came to Japan to suffer for the Japanese people. For a Christian to suffer is not a matter of pain or strain. Jesus suffered more than any other man. The Christian believer is not afraid to suffer with or like Christ. Yes, you have helped me to understand this. "

The Governor shook hands in European style with the slim, disheveled priest. There were tears in his eyes. "Go and continue to preach your religion," he said.

Before leaving the prison, Fr. Arrupe said, "Goodbye" to the guards. On January 12, 1942, he walked out of the prison. He had been incarcerated for 30 days.

He was greeted at the rectory with many hugs. Many of the parishioners had been interrogated by the Kempeitai during Arrupe's imprisonment. Thereafter, his care and support not only from the parishioners but also from the prison guards whom he would see on the streets of Yamaguchi was most warm. Remarkably, some of the soldier-guards would come over to the rectory to visit their former prisoner and to play ping-pong with the boys from his parish in the parish hall.

# 4 NOVICE-MASTER

O N MARCH 6, 1942, Father LaSalle, the Superior for the Jesuits in Japan visited Yamaguchi and asked Fr. Arrupe to serve as Novice-Master for the Jesuits in Japan.

Citing his own lack of mastery of Japanese and his as yet meagre acquaintance with the psychology of the Japanese people, Arrupe pleaded his own lack of qualification. Fr. LaSalle was unpersuaded.

On March 11, Pedro received a telegram missioning him to Hiroshima, the site of the Jesuit Novitiate in Japan. He was to come immediately, taking with him his bare necessities. The present Novice-Master was ill and was not able to continue.

In a great hurry, his parishioners organized a farewell party with speeches, singing, dancing and the inevitable cups of teas, yellow and bitter, which can never be missing from any Japanese party. When it was his turn to speak, there was a lump in his throat. He realized how close were the ties between the Japanese people and their priest.

Hiroshima, 141 kilometers from Yamaguchi, was then a city with 400,000 inhabitants. The city had been founded by Taumoto Mori, who built his castle on the great island of Hero Shima. The Jesuits' presence there dates back to 1600 when Fr. Celso Confaloneri founded a Jesuit residence in Hiroshima. In 1614, a religious persecution of Christians would end the Jesuit presence there for a long period.

In 1908, the Pope asked Jesuits to found a university in Japan. So Sophia University was founded. In 1933, a Jesuit Novitiate was located at that site, but in 1938 it was moved to Nagatsuka, a town on the outskirts of the city of Hiroshima. During World War II, the building where the novitiate was located also served as a residence for a small number of Jesuit seminarians studying philosophy and theology.

Nagatsuka is situated in a scenic mountainous area, a few miles outside the city of Hiroshima. As Arrupe made his way to the site, he passed the grounds of the Night of Lotus Buddhist Temple, belonging to the Jodo Shursa sect. Shortly, he came to what looked like another

Buddhist Temple, a wooden building complete with pointed roofs and a pagoda of three floors and a bell tower topped with a cross. He rang the bell and was greeted by Brother Gropper, S.J., who had started building the Novitiate in 1937 and finished it in 1939.

Not long after he arrived, the *Kempeitai*, who kept vigilance on all foreigners, especially one who had already been imprisoned, came to the Novitiate. The buildings of the Novitiate intrigued them: "Why the three story pagoda-like tower? ...To look over Hiroshima or to install radio-transmitting equipment!!"

"No," Arrupe replied, "all Churches have towers. If the intent was to spy on Hiroshima, the tower would have been built on top of a hill, not in a hollow, 25 meters below."

Even so, they searched the tower, but found nothing—not even dust!

As he began this new assignment, Arrupe realized that to teach spirituality to his Japanese novices, he needed to know more than the Japanese language. He would have to know and appreciate their culture. He became obsessed with knowing all about Japanese people and Japanese culture from inside. Within a few days of his arrival, he arranged with Kato-san, a master of *chawan* (tea ceremonies), to take private lessons. The tea ceremony was regarded as one of the means of getting insight into a person's inner soul.

Pedro would bicycle twice a week down across Nagatsuka to meet with Kato-san, who would greet him with a bow and a smile. They would go through the ritual, which consisted of doing something simple, but with great solemnity, with measured bows and gestures. After a few weeks, Arrupe asked Kato-san if he would soon be able to do the ceremony. "Maybe in three years, you will know the essentials," the tea professor smiled.

Arrupe learned that achieving peace and enlightenment through finding one's inner soul, in Japanese culture, is facilitated not only by the tea ceremony, but also by *shado* (calligraphy) and by *bado* (the art of firing the arrow). So Arrupe began to spend one hour a day in *fude* (painting Japanese characters with a brush—not only to write, but also to be one with, to identify with, the painted forms). He also took up the bow and arrow. The purpose of this exercise is not so much to concentrate on hitting the target as to focus on the slow, deliberate action of drawing back the bow and slowly releasing the arrow at a straw target with great tranquility. Arrupe ardently pursued all these avenues of Japanese inculturation as he worked at his new mission, learning how best to serve as Novice-Master for his Japanese charges.

As the war and its hardships intensified and food became scarcer, Fr. Arrupe's responsibility for the seminarians' care extended to finding food for them. Things, in fact, became so desperate in Nagatsuka that he had to send the philosophy and theology students to Tokyo and to have the novices who remained with him allot the time and energy which in peaceful times would be dedicated to study and formation, to working on the land around the Novitiate to grow food.

His former novices remember him as an extraordinary teacher, filled with good humor. The example of his life was an inspiration. He frequently slept for only four hours. Every day without exception, he would start the day with a "Holy Hour" in the Chapel near the Tabernacle. Each morning, he would spend one hour in meditation, sitting in Zen fashion, immobile on his heels ... Arrupe knew each novice personally and treated each individually, adapting his approach according to different circumstances and personalities and he would often ask forgiveness from his novices.

As the war wore on, teaching the novices became more difficult, not only because of the exigencies of the war, but also because several of those entering the Novitiate were not teenagers but battle-hardened, experienced veterans returning from the front.

A number of the young men in the Novitiate were called to serve in the military and died in combat. The tombs of two of these young men lie in the Novitiate cemetery on the top of a hill overlooking the green valley of Nagatsuka. Some of Arrupe's former novices, however, survived the war and battle, and came back to go on to the priesthood in the Jesuit order. They remembered Fr. Arrupe with much affection.

Fr. Arrupe's stay in Nagatsuka, just outside of the city of Hiroshima, would continue through and beyond the horrible event of August 6, 1945, the dropping of the atomic bomb on Hiroshima.

# 5 Japan Under Siege

N MAY OF 1945, Germany surrendered to the Allies. A similar fate for Japan seemed inevitable. The Japanese no longer had enough food and their fuel reserves were practically exhausted. Many in the country were ready to capitulate. Foreign Minister Tojo had admitted that "Japan is defeated. We must face and act accordingly." The Emperor himself was in favor of peace initiatives.

But it was the military that were the power behind the Japanese throne. The Emperor was nothing but a front for the military authorities, the *Gumbutsu*. The Emperor's role was to reign, not rule. From the very outset of Japan's incursion into Mantua area, China, and East Asia, the military had presented themselves as the natural leaders and liberators of the region from "the British and American imperialists."

The initial success of the Japanese attacks and conquests—Pearl Harbor, the Philippine Islands, Hong Kong, British Borneo, all of Southeast Asia, the Caroline Islands, New Guinea—made the military's claims seem incontrovertible. And the war had been so remote from Japan itself that it had made no impact on the ordinary person.

But then in 1943 and 1944, the Allied forces advanced across the Pacific in a series of gigantic steps from island to island. These islands would be used to enable US bombers to attack the Japanese homeland. With the conquest of Saipan, U.S. B–29 bombers began to bomb sixty-six major Japanese cities.

The military dictatorship duped the Japanese people into believing that the setbacks where the price of a future victory that would ultimately be won. The high price of casualties inflicted on the Americans would ultimately, as the war came closer to Japan, serve in Japan's favor and final victory would be theirs. Preservation of the national honor demanded nothing less than a fight to the last man. To the Gumbutsu, surrender was unthinkable. Instead of surrender, the Supreme Command issued the following resolution:

> With a faith born of eternal loyalty as our inspiration, we shall, thanks to the advantage of our terrain and the loyalty of our people, prosecute the war to the bitter end, to uphold our national essence (*Kobutai*), protect the Imperial land, and achieve our goals of conquest.

Because the Emperor remained silent it was assumed that he approved, and plans for "Operation Decisive," the decisive battle on the homeland, were put in hand. The Army continued to insist that it was here that victory would be rested from apparent defeat "even at the cost of a million men."

Ever since May 1945, the American public had been deeply afflicted by the staggering losses suffered by their forces. The battle over Okinawa lasted from April 6 to June 21, and cost the Americans 12,000 dead. The Japanese fought with incredible tenacity and fanaticism and total contempt for death. More Americans had been killed or wounded in the caves of Okinawa than during the whole campaign for the conquest of the Philippines.

The Japanese tended to idealize death at the expense of life. In some mysterious way, the way a person died seemed to be more important than the way the person lived. A soldier who surrendered was dishonored for the rest of his life and could never return to his native country. (Hence the notorious Japanese contempt for prisoners of war!) It was clear that the Japanese would fight to the bitter end until the last surviving Japanese soldier was dug out of the cave on top of Mount Fuji!

In the face of such perceived intransigence, the U.S. President Harry Truman, under the influence of Gen. Douglas MacArthur directed, on June 1, that an atomic bomb should be released on Japan as soon as possible. MacArthur, the General in charge of the Allied Army, had proposed that as the military invasion of Japan would cost a minimum of 2 million Japanese lives and 1 million American and Allied lives, and as the use of the atomic bomb would entail the sacrifice of only possibly 250,000 Japanese lives; therefore, the bomb should be dropped.

The committee advising Truman on this issue, after much soul-searching, had unanimously recommended such a move as soon as possible in these words:

> To extract a genuine surrender from the Emperor and his military advisers, they must be administered a tremendous shock that would carry convincing proof of our power to destroy the Empire. Such a shock would save many times the number of lives (both American and Japanese) than it would cost.

The committee agreed that they should first try to persuade Japan to surrender by warning her in the strongest possible way of the consequences if she did not.

So, on July 27, 1945, an ultimatum was delivered to Tokyo threatening *"total and utter destruction"* if all Japanese forces did not unconditionally surrender. Though the Japanese Prime Minister Suzuki was himself desperate for peace, but a peace that would protect the Emperor, he was overruled by the cabinet and military leaders and, on July 28, sent back Japan's refusal.

# 6 Pika-Don

THE ALLIED FORCES then set about arranging the mission to drop an atomic bomb. For a variety of reasons, *Hiroshima* was chosen as the first target though warnings had also been sent to the cities of Kokura and Nagasaki.

On August 6, 1945, the Enola Gay, carrying the atomic bomb, and two companion super fortresses, one with camera and photographic equipment, the other with tactical and scientific equipment, took off from Tinian Island at 1:37 a.m. They would arrive at Hiroshima at 8:10 a.m. Two days earlier, American B-29's had dropped thousands of leaflets on the city, warning the people that if Japan did not surrender, the city would be destroyed by a bomb too horrendous to contemplate. The inhabitants should evacuate the city ...The people ignored this as just propaganda!

August 6, 1945. That morning, Father Arrupe had just entered his study at 8:10 AM. On the wall in front of his desk was a crucifix, and a timepiece. He still had some minutes before class.

But he didn't. For at that instant, a blinding light, like burning magnesium in a photographer's flashbulb, dazzling as a bolt of lightning, filled the room. There was no sound. Everything seemed to stop; the world seemed to be in a state of suspended animation.

It was the Feast of the Transfiguration of our Lord. That very morning at Mass, Father Arrupe had read Matthew's account:

> Jesus took with him Peter, James, and John, and led them up a high mountain. There he was transfigured before them. His face shone like the sun, and his clothes became as white as the light. Then a bright cloud enveloped them, and a voice from the cloud said, "This is my Son, whom I love; with Him, I am well pleased. Listen to him!" When the disciples heard this, they fell face-down to the ground, terrified. But Jesus came and touched them. "Get up," He said, "don't be afraid." (Mt 17:1,-2, 5–7)

Arrupe jumped up to see what was happening. As he opened the door that faced the city of Hiroshima, a tremendous explosion shattered his eardrums. A blast of hot air sent him crashing to the other side of the room, where he collapsed to the floor. Bits of glass, roof tiles, and bricks rained down. A large fragment of glass miraculously missed him and buried itself into the wall opposite him. His *tatami* mat was buried under a foot and a half of plaster, glass, and debris. There was debris everywhere. It was some four or five seconds before he was able to pick himself up. Those few seconds seemed an eternity—when one fears that a beam is about to crash down and crush one's skull at any moment. He looked at the clock. It was still 8:10. The clock's pendulum seemed nailed down... as if to record for posterity the time of birth of man's ultimate weapon of mass destruction.

It slowly dawned on Father Arrupe that a monster bomb had exploded directly over the house. He rushed through the rest of the building. He now had direct responsibility for 35 young men studying for the priesthood, many of whom most recently have been evacuated from the Tokyo seminary to the comparative—until now—safety of the Hiroshima seminary. Sitting in the hallway was a dazed German priest, a book still in his hands. A few seconds earlier, he had been resting against the window-sill of his room several meters away. The priest was no small man; he weighed well over 200 pounds. Everything was in a state of confusion. All the windows had been smashed and all the doors forced inward; all the bookshelves had tumbled down and books were strewn everywhere. Some of the novices and priests were bleeding from fragments of glass, but none was seriously injured. No one seemed to have come to serious harm.

Arrupe went with some other Jesuits into the garden to see where the bomb had fallen. They stared at each other in total disbelief; there was no crater in the ground anywhere; there was no sign of an explosion. The trees and flowers were all quite fresh and normal. But it was surely a bomb. They ventured into the rice-fields surrounding the house, looking for where the bomb had landed. But again there was no hole or sign of any explosion yet not a door or window remained in place. At least the main building still stood—another credit to the building skills of Brother Gropper.

They then looked across to the city. Dense columns of black smoke rose to the heavens; enormous flames leapt into the sky, accompanied by the sound of smaller explosions. They concluded an incendiary bomb with an especially strong explosive action had struck the city. Down in the valley about a mile away, several peasant houses were on fire and the woods on the opposite side of the valley were aflame. They climbed the hill to get a better view. They could not believe their eyes. Below them lay a city totally annihilated, 100,000 souls had vanished into oblivion—dead before they knew it. The city was flaming red; a huge mushroom-like cloud billowed up into the sky.

It seemed the epicenter of the explosion had been at Yokogawa Station, 2 miles away. The Jesuit mission and parish house was there in the center of the city. Four priests lived there: Father LaSalle ,the superior, Father Kleinsorge, Father Cieslik, and Father Schiffer. Also living there were a Japanese fourth-year theology student, Takemoto, and the secretary to the diocese, Kanji Fukai, who had been an Anglican priest before converting to Catholicism. The community at the Novitiate wondered about the fate of Father Superior LaSalle and the other Fathers and parishioners there. They were also concerned about Father Kopp who had left early that morning to say mass at the Shudoin Orphanage for children, run by the Sisters of the Poor, on the edge of the city. There was no news of him or the Sisters. However Father Kopp and the Sisters arrived later that afternoon. Father Kopp was bleeding profusely from the head and neck and had a large burn on his right palm. They had picked their way along the shore of the river and through the burning streets. The Orphanage, built by Brother Gropper, had withstood the first blast, but being built of wood was unable to resist the flames and had burned to the ground, along with the entire district. There was no water available anywhere to curb the fires.

About half an hour after the explosion, a procession of people getting thicker by the minute, began to stream up the valley. They were fleeing the burning city. They were unable to run; the horrific injuries they had sustained made sure of that. Most were bleeding profusely or suffering from severe burns. Many displayed horrible wounds of the extremities and back. The less seriously injured carried the more serious victims on their backs. A group of young women, 18 to 20 years old, clung to one another as they dragged themselves along the road. One had a blister that covered her entire chest, burns across her face, and a gaping cut in her scalp probably caused by a falling tile; blood coursed down her face.

The priests converted their beautiful chapel into a temporary hospital, taking in about 50 of the most wounded refugees. It was fortunate that Father Arrupe was a doctor. He rushed into the house to rescue any medical supplies. He found a medical chest under some rubble. He was able to retrieve some iodine, some aspirin tablets and some bicarbonate of soda. These were the only medications available to hundreds crying out desperately for medical help. The priests gave what first aid they could. The quantities of fat so carefully saved up during the lean years of the war were soon used up in treating the burns. Underclothing, sheets, anything at hand was torn up to make bandages. Soon there were no drugs left; all they could do was clean up the wounds. Meanwhile the chapel and library and any other available rooms were cleared of broken glass and debris and used as an emergency casualty clearing station, the dying being placed on mats of straw. But very soon the makeshift hospital had reached its capacity of 150 beds. It could take no more. The other unfortunates had to lie down in the garden, in the fields, in the road—wherever they could find space.

The wounded—those who could utter any sounds—kept muttering the words '*Pika-Don.*' They had seen a brilliant greenish white flash of light (*Pika*), like the sunlight at noon multiplied endless times, followed by a tremendous explosion (*Don*) that sounded as if it would pound your body to pieces. *Pika-Don* (*flash-bang; lightning-thunder*) was their name for the devastating bomb.

In addition to medicine, what the injured needed was food to provide the energy needed to combat the hemorrhages, fever, and infection caused by the severe burns. So on foot or on bicycle the young men of the house scoured the outskirts of Hiroshima to procure the lifesaving food. Without wondering how or from where, these young fellows came back with more fish, meat, eggs, and butter than had been seen in four years. Many carefully tended gardens were sadly depleted having only squashes and potatoes. This food, however, provided the sustenance to fight the anemia and leukemia that would develop in the majority of those exposed to atomic radiation. Father Stolte and Father Erlinghaven ventured down the road to the village of Nagatsuka. The road was full of refugees. They brought into a temporary aid station the seriously injured who had fallen by the wayside. There, iodine was applied to the wounds, but they were left unclean as no other medications were available. Those who had been brought in were laid on the floor and no one could give them any further care.

At about 4 o'clock in the afternoon, Brother Takemoto arrived with two kindergarten children who lived in the parish house in the center of the city. He reported that the church, the house and all the adjoining buildings had been burned down. He also reported that Father Superior LaSalle and Father Schiffer had been seriously injured. They had taken refuge in Asano Park, on the river bank. They were too weak and injured to move.

At 5 o'clock, Father Arrupe and some of his colleagues decided that despite the danger to themselves—for any foreigners would be suspected of being spies who had connived with the enemy in this air attack—they must go into Hiroshima to give what assistance they could. They hastily made two stretchers out of poles and boards, collected together some food and medicines and made for the devastated city, with Brother Takemoto showing the way. They first called in at the aid station at the village school where Father Arrupe was able to give some medical advice and assistance. The mayor of Nagatsuka was organizing the distribution of balls of white rice to the wounded. But the charnel-house smell was so strong that few were hungry.

The once-green paddy-fields near Nagatsuka were now streaked with brown. All the houses still standing had their roofs off and broken doors and windows. But then the scenery changed suddenly. Everything was a brown scar; every house had been buffeted down or burned. Along the way, there were men, women and children, dead and dying and begging for help. Frightfully burned people, the skin peeling off from the shoulders so that it hung from their fingertips, screamed for help.

Ohshiba Park was like a battlefield, full of groaning and wounded. People were rolling about in agony, even on top of the people burned too badly to move.

As they got near to where the city center had once stood, the macabre scene beggared the imagination. Before them lay a city flattened, except here and there, a few concrete buildings, like tombstones in a vast fire-swept cemetery, steel girders melted, a waste-land as far as the eye could see, not a plant or tree or house standing ... They couldn't get nearer the center of the city, which was still a sea of flames, burning with a frightful roaring sound, as though gunpowder had caught fire. There were flames everywhere. The city's water mains had been split open and could provide no pressure. All water and electricity were cut off. The whole area was one huge bonfire.

They followed the twisted and tangled tracks of street-cars, still burning hot and dangerous, to help give them their bearings. The asphalt on the streets was still soft from the heat; walking was difficult. The streets were cluttered with parts of the houses and stores that had slid into them. They clambered over the hot smoking roofs, their occupants pinned under the buildings and buried alive. From every second or third house came the screams of people trapped and abandoned, pleading for help, ... but within their agony they never lost their politeness: "Help, if you please!" they cried.

It was difficult to make headway against the fleeting thousands. A woman her body all greasy and purple like an eggplant all covered with blood, her hair red-brown and frizzled, ran past calling out her child's name, '*Hanako-chan!*" "*Hanako-chan!*" A mother lay face downward, tightly holding her dead baby with one arm and groaning pitifully. Children were calling the names of their fathers and mothers and brothers and sisters. The cries "mommy" and "daddy" were everywhere. A man shouting "*Shinzi! Shinzi!*" limped past, calling for his lost child.

Sight of those badly burned by the hot breath of the atomic blasts was beyond imagination. Some had been burned to a cinder standing up. Others had literally been roasted alive. Those who had survived were wrapped in what looked like wisps of smoke—the smoke was their skin peeling off from their bodies in red strips.... Many had their eyes so swollen that they couldn't see, and were staggering around like blind people, groups of them colliding with each other and falling down.

"*Mizu, mizu!*—find me water please!" People, their faces so bloated or burned beyond recognition were begging: "Water! Water!"!

Suddenly, the path of the Jesuits was blocked. The whole street was aflame with a block of fallen houses. They made for a bridge that would take them across the Kyobashi River ... The river was crowded with people some standing, some crouching, some lying in the shallows taking refuge in the cool water. Those who quenched their thirst from the river were nauseated and soon began vomiting. Others were nauseated but they thought it was not because of the water but because of the gas given off by the bomb. There was a strong odor of ionization, an electric smell, caused by the bomb's fusion.

Understandably, many people had become insane. One man seriously burned and in tatters walked up and down proclaiming: "I am a general of the Army."

There was no road to walk—just the top of roofs under which the red embers still burned. They tiptoed then their way between the roof tiles and the flames. Choju Park was littered with the dead and dying. They tiptoed over or side-stepped the prostrate forms and eventually reached the river embankment. They made their way along the river bank between the burning and smoking ruins; more often they were forced by heat and smoke at the level of the street, to wade into the river itself.

Eventually they came upon their colleagues in the far corner of Asano Park. The park was like a battlefield with rank on rank of dead and injured and burned and bleeding lying everywhere, their red black faces staring wildly. It was hard to distinguish the living from the dead, for most of the people lay still, their eyes open.

Their colleagues were lying by the river bank, completely spent. Father Schiffer was stretched out on the ground, as white as a sheet. As there were no bandages, his head was wrapped in newspapers and a shirt, so that he looked like a turbaned merchant from the Orient. Father Arrupe made a quick examination of his seriously injured colleagues. Father Schiffer was in critical condition. In the rush of fleeing the approaching flames at the church, the first aid treatment applied had failed to detect another wound in his outer ear; a piece of glass had penetrated a small artery and he was bleeding to death. The blood was spurting out like red ink from a water pistol. Using some wooden sticks and bamboo planks, they improvised a stretcher for him. Father Schiffer groaned aloud in pain as they laid him on the sticks; then with the stoicism of a true Japanese, the German priest smiled at Father Arrupe and said, "Father, would you please look at my back; I think there is something there!"

They turned him facedown. By the light of a torch they saw that his back was completely covered with wounds made by small pieces of glass. It was difficult to address the wounds properly in the dark. With a razor blade, "Don Pedro," as Fr. Arrupe was known, removed more than 50 fragments.

Father LaSalle was also seriously injured. As the flash had struck, he had twisted away from the window. Long shards of glass had embedded themselves into his exposed back and lower extremity. He had a deep gash in his left leg. He was covered with blood.

A group of soldiers walked past. Suddenly, the officer rushed back, his sword raised in the classic *kindo* position of attack. He heard the group talking in a foreign language and assumed the priests were American parachutists who were reported to have landed. He shouted, demanded to know who they were. He was about to strike down Father Arrupe when Fr. Laures seized him by the arm and explained they were Germans—allies of the Japanese.

The priests discussed how to get Father Schiffer and Father LaSalle out to the novitiate. They were afraid that blundering through the park in the dark would jar them too much on the wooden stretchers they were using, and that the wounded men would lose too much blood.

Father Kleinsorge remembered Mr. Tanimoto and his boat. Mr. Tanimoto was a Methodist pastor. Father Kleinsorge called out to him on the river. When Mr. Tanimoto reached the river bank with his punt, he said he would be glad to take the injured priests and their bearers upstream to where they could find a clearer path. They both decided that Father Schiffer, the more seriously injured, should go first. They put him onto one of the stretchers and lowered it into the boat and two of them went aboard with a stretcher. Mr. Tanimoto, who had no oars, polled the punt upstream.

They carried the stretcher out of the punt, with Brother Takemoto, the theology student leading the way to warn of obstacles and hazards. There were plenty of these—fallen trees, fragments of ruins, wires. In the dark; it was impossible to see them all. Father Kruer (one of the stretcher bearers) got his foot tangled in some telephone wire and tripped, bringing down the litter with him. Father Schiffer fell off and lost consciousness. When he came to, he vomited. The bearers packed him up and then continued even more warily. They would stop every few hundred yards—to relieve the pain of Father Schiffer and also to give the stretcher bearers a rest. The slightest movement caused Father Schiffer agony; he was still losing large quantities of blood.

On the Misai Bridge, they met Fr. Tappe and Fr. Luhmer, who had come from the Novitiate at Nogatsuka to meet them. They had just dug a family out of the ruins of their collapsed house, some 150 yards off the road. They had dragged out two girls and placed them on the side of the road; their father was already dead. Their mother was still trapped under heavy beams. With great effort, they were eventually able to free her. They left Fr. Schiffer with the two newly arrived priests and returned to Asuno Park to get Father Lasalle.

Mr. Tanimoto returned to the priests by the river bank at Asuno Park. He was agitated and excited. He had seen two children standing up to their necks in the river. Would the priests help him to rescue them? A group set off and were able to rescue the two girls who were both badly burned. They had both lost their family. They laid the two girls down on the bank next to Father Lasalle.

Father LaSalle, who was only clad in shirt and trousers, was freezing despite the warm summer night and the heat of the burning city. One of the priests gave up his coat, another his shirt; they were glad to be wearing less in the oppressive heat. They loaded Father Superior on the punt. Father Cieslik thought he could make it to the Novitiate on foot. Father Kleinsorge was too exhausted by now. He decided he would wait in the park until the next day. He asked the men to come back with a handcart so they could take some of the badly injured children to the novitiate.

Mr. Tanimoto took Father LaSalle to the river bank nearest the trail back to the novitiate and then drove his boat to the other side of the river where 20 men and women were calling for help, unable to move as the water began to mount. Mr. Tanimoto put them on the punt despite their awful wounds and took them to a higher location, carrying them up the slope away from the tide.

Meanwhile some other priests had carried Father LaSalle up to the Novitiate. Scores of tiny fragments of window glass still remained embedded in Father LaSalle's back. The journey on the litter constructed out of wooden boards was for him a painful nightmare. Unable to see in the darkness, the litter bearers stumbled into a ditch. Father Lasalle was thrown to the ground; the litter broke in two. They couldn't go any further. One of the priests went ahead to get a handcart from the novitiate. He was lucky; he soon found one beside an empty house and wheeled it back. He lifted Father LaSalle onto the cart and pushed him over the bumpy road the rest of the way.

They reached the Novitiate at 4:30 AM. Father Arrupe was looking for some rest. He didn't get any for someone else was in his bed; he got one half hour sleep on the floor.

In the light of dawn Mr. Tanimoto looked across the river and was horrified to discover the 20 persons he had carried up the slope had drowned; he had not carried them up high enough.

# 7 THE AFTERMATH

O N AUGUST 7, the next day, Father Arrupe celebrated mass at 5 AM in the Novitiate Chapel, which was now filled with the sick and wounded lined all about. He recalled his feelings that morning:

> The chapel, half destroyed, was overflowing with the wounded, who were lying on the floor very near to one another, suffering terribly, twisted with pain. I began the Mass as best I could in the midst of the mass of humanity who had not the slightest idea what was going on at the altar. They were non-Christians and had never attended Mass before. I can never forget the terrible feeling I experienced when I turned toward them and saw this sight from the altar. I could not move. I stayed there as if I was paralyzed, my arms outstretched, contemplating this human tragedy—human science and technological progress used to destroy the human race. They were all looking at me with eyes full of agony and despair as if they were waiting for some consolation to come from the altar. What a terrible scene!
>
> A prayer for those who had the savage cruelty to drop the atomic bomb came spontaneously to my lips: "Lord, pardon them for they know not what they do." And for those lying helpless beside and before me, twisted with pain, "Lord, give them the faith—that they may see; give them strength to bear their pain."
>
> Torrents of graces certainly poured out from that host and from that altar. Six months later when having been cared for, all had left our house (only two persons died); many among them had been baptized and all had learned that Christian charity knows how to understand, help, and give consolation that surpasses all human comfort. This charity had communicated the serenity that helps one to smile in spite of pain and to forgive those who have caused so much suffering.

Several of the priests set off from the Novitiate to give what help they could in the city and its suburbs. One pushed a handcart to bring back anyone too burned or injured to walk. One severely wounded man refused any assistance until he first ascertained the nationality of the helpers; he suspected they might be American paratroopers. In the broad light of day, they could see clearly the extent of the devastation. Dead bodies and carcasses of horses and dogs lay around everywhere. A mother, her baby strapped to her back, had been burned in the debris of her home. Sometimes, it was difficult to pass by the purple, blackened, swollen corpses without treading on them; you would hear the crunch of a shoe or boot on bones. There was plaster and blood and vomit everywhere. The smell was appalling—the priests had to tie cloths over their noses. Fr. Cieslik wrote later that "for more than half a year the disgusting smell of destruction and putrefaction continued to assail our nostrils."

On the way they bumped into Fr. Sanada, who was a parish priest at Kure. He had come to Hiroshima to find out what had happened. He was a lucky man. On the day of the bomb, he went to Kure station to catch the commuter train to Hiroshima. The train arrived at Hiroshima at 8 a.m. but Fr. Sanada was not on it; for the first time in his life, he had been late for a train.

They heard the sound of an aircraft above. No one bothered. There weren't any air-shelters to go to anyway. A young child of about seven ran out from under her temporary home of board and tin roofing, looked up and shouted: "Give me back my sister."

In the distance, from the docks in the south to the foothills in the north, everything they saw had been flattened into a desert of still-smoldering ash. Fr. Cieslik recorded:

> It was an eerie landscape that met my eyes as I walked along the silent streets: the macabre ruins of burnt-out houses against the background of a burn-out plain, stone fences half-collapsed, the bare limbs of burnt trees. The scene was as bleak as I imagined the surface of the moon to be. The only building standing, far downtown, was the towering shell of the Fukuyama Department Store, built to withstand earthquakes.

There were people about—all heads bent, searching, searching in the ruins and ashes for their relatives. Cremation of the dead and enshrinement of their remains is a far greater moral responsibility to the Japanese than care of the living. Solitary survivors bowed low and with great dignity, before some empty, burned plot of ground to honor those who had perished there. A man had found his wife's gold tooth and the bone of her elbow.

New fires were springing up everywhere. These were funeral pyres. Clearance squads collected—rather scraped up—piles of corpses that they then stacked with military precision on top of timbers from gutted houses and then set fire to them according to Japanese custom. The ashes were then put into envelopes, marked with names, wherever possible, and then piled in stacks near the pyres. Soldiers dug big holes, poured the corpses into them, poured kerosene over the cadavers and then set them afire. Later, they would fill in the pit. Bluish flames drifted into the sky. The sickening smell of burning flesh hung everywhere over the city. Chinese convicts, wearing blue armbands, were fishing corpses out of the river with what looked like harpoons. They hoisted them onto an iron roasting grill, as if fish to be cooked. A few devout persons carried straw sandals with black and white straps to place on the feet of the corpses of their loved ones before cremation. Other devout Japanese were tearfully collecting up the ashes of burnt relatives and putting them in urns which they would cradle in their arms as they took them to where the Temple had once stood. A few had improvised coffins into which they put the bodies, along with home-make cakes for the dead person's next life.

As they got nearer the city center, Hiroshima became more and more a silent graveyard, filled only with the mute protest of the ruins. Everything stank of sulfur and dead bodies. Here and there, on tile or a pile of ashes, messages were left: "Sister, where are you?" or "All safe and we are at Toyosaka." The priests went to where the Mission House had stood and retrieved some suitcases that had been stored in the air-raid shelter and also the remains of melted chalices and patens in the ashes of the chapel.

At about noon, they reached Asano Park. Fr. Kleinsorge was busy fetching water for the wounded in a bottle and teapot he had borrowed. There was a tap outside the gate of the park. He stepped carefully through the rock gardens and climbed over and crawled under the trunks of fallen trees. On his return, he lost his way. He passed a group of soldiers, their faces wholly burned, their eye-sockets hollow; fluid from their melted eyes had run down their cheeks. They could have been anti-aircraft gunners gazing upward when the bomb exploded.

Feeding the water to the seriously burned was difficult. Some had their mouths so swollen and deformed that they couldn't open them. He procured a large piece of grass, drew out the end to make a drinking straw, and helped them to drink that way. A brother and sister aged five and thirteen had befriended him. Their name was Katoka. They had just set out for school when the bomb fell. They joined their mother in the evacuation station at Asano Park. Their mother decided to go home for food and clothing. They had not seen her since. The two accompanied Fr. Kleinsorge and Fr. Nobuhra back to the Novitiate. They were inconsolable, sure they would never see their mother again. Fr. Cieslik tried to console them as best he could by playing games with them, asking them riddles such as "what is the cleverest animal in the world?" They would guess "an ape," "an elephant" and so on.

"No. It's a hippo!" came the answer because in Japanese, a hippopotamus is '*kaba*,' which is the reverse of '*baka*,' which means 'stupid.' Or, he would entertain them with '*Kami-shibai*,' story-shows making funny drawings on paper and imitating the noises of animals. Several days later, the children were reunited with their mother as a result of messages left on a board in the Ujina post office.

By now, the Novitiate had been transformed into an emergency hospital. The former University of Madrid medical student *Don Pedro* Arrupe was now priest-turned-doctor. Since the early morning Mass, he had begun treating the sick and injured and burned and mentally confused and despairing, who were everywhere ... in the chapel, in the corridors, in the garden. Fr. Arrupe had no medicines or equipment, no anesthetics, not even '*naucopon*,' the Japanese sedative. He used his desk as an operating table. He performed the surgical operations without any anesthetic, cutting away the flesh with plain household scissors. They tore up underwear and shirts and sheets to make bandages.

One young boy had a piece of glass, shaped like a fishtail, stuck into the pupil of his left eye. Some of the priests and his fellow students held the boy's head while Fr. Arupe removed the glass without causing more damage. The little fellow was begging Don Pedro to stop.

"*Gambari! Gambari* (Be brave!)," the priest-doctor kept saying. Just then there was a blinding flash as a gas storage tank blew up. The boy didn't blink. He was blind.

A man had a shard of glass sticking into his back. He had ripped his bare hands trying to extract the glass stiletto. A child, with a large wooden splinter protruding like a dagger from between his ribs, called out "*Shimpu-sana* (Father) save me."

At eight o'clock one of the workmen of the Novitiate arrived carrying a sack on his head. "Father, I came upon this sack filled with little bottles that look like medicine." They were phials of boric acid. This providential discovery of thirty pounds of antiseptic was to save many lives and lessen the pain of countless others.

Father Arrupe had the intuition that the best way to heal the radiation burns was to give nature a chance to work unimpeded. So, all he did was to clean the wounds and disinfect them with boric acid compresses. A solution of the antiseptic would be placed on the improvised bandages that were then placed on the wounds. The antiseptic solution would keep the lesions moist all day and in contact with the air. In this way the wounds were kept clean and the pain lessened. The discharge from the wounds would adhere to the dressing and by changing it four or five times a day, asepsis was assured. In a few-days-time, a scar would begin to form which would slowly bring about total healing. (If the wound was not kept constantly clean, blood-poisoning was sure to set in.) The result was beyond all expectations. Of the ninety people treated at the Novitiate, some of whom had very severe burns and injuries, only one died. He was a nine-year-old boy, who died not of burns, but of inflammation of the brain membrane.

For months, Father Arrupe and the priests-turned-medical-orderlies were kept busy tending the sick and wounded. This was a task they performed day and night, non-stop, catching snippets of sleep whenever they could. There was no one else to do the jobs of cleaning, wiping, daubing, and winding.

Father Siemes recorded: "Our work was, in the eyes of the people, a greater boost to Christianity than all our work during the preceding long years."

Some years later, Father Arrupe was visited by a young Japanese priest, Father Hasegawa. He was one of those whose festering wounds, the effect of infrared radiation, had been treated by Arrupe. He was later baptized by him.

Of the 260 doctors in the city before the explosion, 200 had perished. Of the 60 that remained, many were wounded. Father Arrupe himself had found the Director of the Red Cross Hospital buried under the ruins of his house and had rescued him. He had six bone fractures and was in no state to help anyone.

Of the 1,780 nurses, 1,654 were dead or too badly injured to work. Some untrained persons jumped into the breech but sadly their assistance was often misplaced and injurious. They placed on wounds mercurochrome, the only 'medicine' available. It did not heal but caused the destruction of body tissues. They also used turnip pulp, or oil such as fish oil. These home-made remedies might help at first but in the long-run caused severe bodily damage. Father Arrupe and his assistants went from house to house telling people that these homemade cures spelled certain death and taught them a safer healing process.

Father Arrupe recorded later his experience of those horrendous days:

> Among all the cases we treated, perhaps those that caused the most suffering were the children. At the time of the atomic bomb, most of the children were in their respective schools. For that reason, during the explosion, thousands of children were separated from their parents; many were wounded and cast into the streets without being able to fend for themselves. We brought all we could to Nagatsuka and began treating them immediately so as to prevent infection and fever.

We had absolutely no anesthetics and some of the children were horribly wounded. One had a cut from ear to ear as a result of a beam that fell on his head. The edge of the wound was one and a half centimeters wide; the injured region of the scalp was filled with clay and pieces of glass. The screams of the poor child during his treatment so upset the entire house that we had no choice but to tie him into a cart with sheets and take him to the top of the hillock near the house. That spot was converted into an amphitheatre where we could work, and the child could scream all he wanted without making everyone a nervous wreck.

Our hearts were torn apart during these treatments, but greater was the consolation at being able to restore the children to their parents. Through the Japanese police, who were well organized, we were able to contact all the families whose children we had in the house.

Memorable are those scenes of reunion with children that were thought dead in the explosion, and now were found alive and well, or at least in the process of healing. Those mothers and fathers, overcome with joy, did not know how to express their gratitude, throwing themselves at our feet.

Until the day after the explosion, we did not know that we were dealing with the first atomic bomb to explode in the world. At first, without electricity or radio, we were cut off from the world. The following day, cars and trains began arriving from Tokyo and Saka with help for Hiroshima ...[1]

People were warned not to enter the city, because there was gas in the air "that kills for seventy years." Arrupe reflected that when one knows there are 50,000 bodies which, unless they are cremated, will cause a terrible plague, and also some 120,000 wounded to care for, a priest cannot preserve his own life. When one is told that in the city there is a gas that kills, one must be very determined to ignore the fact and go

---

[1]   Cf. Pedro Arrupe," Surviving the Atomic Bomb" in Michael Glazier, *Recollections and Reflections by Pedro Arrupe*, S.J., pp. 34–36.

in. And he did. He records what he discovered when he entered the "forbidden city":

> I remember a Japanese girl of around eighteen whom I had baptized three or four years earlier and who had become a fervent Christian. Every day, she received Communion at the 6:30 Mass in the morning, which she promptly attended every day. One day after the explosion of the atomic bomb, I was passing through the streets clogged with masses of ruins of every kind. On the spot where her house had formerly stood, I found a kind of hut supported by some poles and covered with pieces of tin. I went up to it. A wall about a foot and a half high marked off a place within its interior. I tried to enter but an unbearable stench repelled me. The young Christian, her name was Nakamura, was lying on a rough table raised a bit above ground. Her arms and her legs were extended and covered with some burned rags. Her four limbs had become along their whole length a single sore from which pus was oozing and falling down upon and penetrating the earth. Her burned flesh seemed to be little else but bones and wounds.
>
> She had been in this state for thirteen days without being able to take care of herself or clean herself, and she had only eaten a little rice which her father, who was also seriously injured, gave her. Her back was already one gangrenous mass since she had not been able to change her position. When I sought to clean her burns, I found that the muscles were rotten and transformed into pus that left a hollow into which my hand entered and at the bottom of which were a mass of worms.
>
> Appalled by such a terrible sight, I remained without speaking. After a little, Nakamura opened her eyes and when she saw me near and smiling at her, she looked at me with two tears in her eyes and sought to give me her hand which was only a purulent stump and she said to me with a tone that I shall never forget: "Father, have you brought me Communion?" What a Communion that was, so different from that which I had given her each day for so many years! Forgetting all her sufferings, all here desires for physical relief, Nakamura asked me for what she had continued to desire for two weeks, from the day on which the atom bomb

exploded. She asked for the Eucharist, for Jesus Christ, her great consoler, to whom she had months earlier offered her body and soul to work for the poor as a religious. I would have given anything to have been able to hear her speak of that experience, of her lack of the Eucharist and of her joy at receiving it after so much suffering. Never before had I experienced such a request from one who had been so cruelly reduced to a "wound and ulcer," nor such Viaticum received with such an intense desire. Nakamura San died soon after, but she had been able to receive and embrace Jesus whom she loved so much and who was anxiously waiting to receive her forever in His home in heaven. I have frequently thought of that scene of Nakamura San. How much she taught me![2]

The priests from the Novitiate went into Hiroshima to find bodies and cremate them. They sifted the ruins of houses, to find whole families crushed beneath; they prevailed upon passers-by to raise pyramids of 50 to 60 bodies at a time and pour fuel on them to set them afire. With the August sun and the humid heat, it was soon easy to know where the bodies lay, by using only the sense of smell. In this way, the bodies dug out from the ruins or abandoned on the streets gradually disappeared.

For the first few hours after the catastrophe in Hiroshima, no one in Tokyo knew what had happened. Tokyo's first knowledge of the disaster at Hiroshima came from a public announcement from the White House in Washington, sixteen hours after the city had been struck ... At dawn on August 7, General Kawabe, the Deputy Chief of General Staff, received a report that was totally incomprehensible to him: "The whole city of Hiroshima was destroyed by a single bomb." The Jesuits in Tokyo offered Requiem Masses for the repose of their colleagues in Hiroshima.

President Harry Truman heard the news of Hiroshima at lunchtime on August 6 while returning from the Potsdam Conference on the cruiser Augusta. He broadcast another—still more urgent—plea to Japan to surrender:

---

[2]    Cf. Pedro Arrupe, S.J., *Justice with Faith Today*, 1981, pp. 296–297.

> Sixteen hours ago, an American airplane dropped one bomb in Hiroshima, Japan, and destroyed its usefulness to the enemy. That bomb had more power than 20,000 tons of TNT. It had more than 2000 times the blast power of the British Grand Slam, which is the largest bomb ever used in the history of warfare. It is an atomic bomb. It is a harnessing of the basic power of the universe. The force from which the sun draws it power has been loosed against those who brought war to the Far East. It was to spare the Japanese people from utter destruction that the ultimatum of the 27th was issued at Potsdam. If they do not now accept our terms, they may expect a rain of ruin from the air, the like of which has never been seen on the earth.

The Japanese leaders did not accept this ultimatum. The majority of Japanese people had not the slightest idea of what the word "atomic" meant. They took Truman's dramatic announcement as just another propaganda ploy.

Again, leaflets were dropped, advising the population to evacuate the next target areas of Kokura and Nagasaki. Some leaflets were even put to rhyme: "In April, Nagasaki was all flowers; in August, it will be flame showers."

People were forbidden to read the leaflets. Those who did regarded them as so much propaganda and dismissed them.

Waiting on the runway at the Tinian airfield was Bock's Car, a Superfortress that was about to deliver a second atom bomb on Japan. The bomb dropped on Hiroshima had been a uranium atom bomb. The bomb to be used via Bock's Car was of plutonium. Such a bomb had been successfully tested less than a month earlier at Alamogordo, in New Mexico.[3]

---

[3]    This second attack had been originally planned for August 20. Then the date was brought forward by nine days to August 11. But a five-day spell of bad weather was forecast beginning on August 10. Then on August 8, Russia declared war on Japan. If Russia was at war with Japan, she could claim part of the spoils of victory. To deny her these, it was decided to bring forward the date of the attack to August 9. Not only would that prevent the Soviets from claiming a real part in the victory over Japan, it might even warn the Russian giant of the future dangers of too ambitious and voracious an appetite. Since the end of the

## The Aftermath

Bock's Car took off early on August 9. Its primary target was Kokua and its huge army arsenal. Its alternative target was Nagasaki, a much larger city than Kokura, and the home of the Mitsubishi factory that produced the torpedoes used in the attack on Pearl Harbor. When the plane reach Kokura, the city was completely hidden under clouds. The pilot had strict orders to bomb only if the target was completely visible. As the plane came toward Nagasaki, there was a break in the clouds. It was over three kilometers northwest of the planned drop. It was exactly 11 a.m. The bombardier released the bomb. It went plummeting down onto the city of 200,00 people. At 11:02, it detonated at 1,500 feet above the Urakami district, where the factories, schools and residences were concentrated. The detonation of the bomb generated a fireball of destruction that carbonized 35,000 people instantly and flattened the center of the city. A total of 70,000 people died. But the extent of the damage was contained because an 800 foot ridge of hills protected the militarily more important district of the city. The damage in Nagasaki was only about a quarter as effective as in *Hiroshima*.

---

War in Europe, the activities of the Soviet Government in the Eastern European countries, especially Poland, had made it abundantly clear that Stalin had no intention of complying with earlier agreements with the Western Allies, and was bent on bringing Eastern Europe into the Soviet bloc.)

# 8 SURRENDER

A T 11 AM on August 9, 1945, just as the second atomic bomb was hurtling through the sky to wreak its horrendous havoc, the six members of the Japanese Supreme Council of War sat down to discuss the surrender demands of the Potsdam Conference in the light of what had happened at Hiroshima. The arguments between the militarists and the peace faction waxed to and fro, between the protagonists of war and of peace. Foreign Minister Togo, backed by the Prime Minister Suzuki and the Navy Minister Admiral Yonai argued that Japan had no choice but to accept the Potsdam terms of surrender. The other three were the War minister, General Anami, Army Chief, General Umezu and Navy Chief, Admiral Toyoda. War Minister Anami would not accept that the Imperial Army would ever surrender; they must fight to the end—to "find life in death." The commanders of the Pacific Islands recaptured by the Americans had ordered their men to fight to the very last drop of blood and had then almost all themselves committed ceremonial *hara-kiri*. How could the defenders of the home islands betray such an example! Japan could not be ringed by battleships and was over 90 percent mountain. The Americans might land on the coastal plains but the Imperial Army and the adult population would fall back to the next mountain and to the next. The Americans would have to fight for years and lose millions of men—or drop those "unconditional surrender" terms with the blasphemous possibility of trying and executing the Emperor. Every Japanese would die a thousand deaths rather than allow that.

The deadlock of the meeting was hopeless, and it was adjourned without any decision.

Some hours later, the news of the bomb on Nagasaki was received. The Emperor summoned the Supreme War Council, all cabinet ministers, and high imperial officials to meet him at midnight in his air-raid shelter. The two factions were prepared to continue their arguments. Admiral Suzuki wearily suggested they should ask the

Emperor to express his wishes. The Emperor did. Small, round-shouldered, near-sighted and very shy, the Emperor began in a piping, almost expressionless voice: he denounced the futility of "prolongation of the bloodshed and cruelty." He agreed that the terms of Potsdam, calling for the disarming of the armed forces and the punishment of war leaders were "unbearable." "Nevertheless," he added, "the time has come when we must bear the unbearable."

Ministers began to sob; the Emperor wiped his cheeks with white gloved hands. He would make an address to the nation at noon, the next morning, August 15, 1945.

During the night, an assassination attempt, led by Major Kari Hatmaka, a fanatical army staff officer, was made on the life of the Emperor, so that he could not broadcast a surrender. But the plot did not succeed. On the morning of the 15th, "announcement teams" of military policemen drove over the acres in Hiroshima and Nagasaki and also through other cities and towns of Japan announcing:

> Attention everyone! Attention! Today at 12 noon, the Emperor
> in person will make an important announcement over the radio.
> All who are capable of moving should make their way to the
> railway station (or some other prominent location) where the
> Emperor's speech will be relayed over the loudspeaker system.

Just before noon, a lieutenant called "Attention!"; and everyone in the NHK studio in Tokyo arose. The officer announced: "This will be a broadcast of the gravest importance. Will all listeners arise."

Soldiers stood stiffly to attention, young civilians lowered their heads; the older knelt to the ground, their faces almost touching the dust, as a nervous, reedy, high-pitched monotone voice they had never heard before, trembled, as if on the verge of tears. It was their Emperor and High Priest of Shinto, speaking from the Chrysanthemum Throne. He began to deliver, in the accent of the court of Japan, the shocking news of the defeat. Many were expecting Tenno, the Emperor, to announce final victory:

> After pondering deeply the general trends of the world, and
> the actual conditions obtaining in Our Empire ... and since

Russia has entered the war and since America had those terrible weapons of destruction ... and since I feel responsible for the lives of 84 million ... in order to avoid further bloodshed, perhaps even the total extinction of civilization ... We have decided to effect a settlement of the present situation by resorting to an extraordinary measure .... We have ordered our Government to communicate with the Governments of the United States, Great Britain and the Soviet Union that the Empire accepts the provisions of the Potsdam Joint Convention.

The terms of the Declaration had demanded unconditional surrender ...Tears of agonized disbelief were shed by the civilian and military in Japan and by the soldiers guarding a crumbling Empire.[1]

The sudden shock of defeat was too much to bear. A vast crowd had gathered in front of the Imperial Palace in Tokyo. In the outpouring of national sorrow, the crowd paid little attention to those zealous army officers who chose to commit *hari-kiri* rather than accept the share of their country's first military defeat in more than two and a half thousand years. The radio blared '*Kimi ga yo,*' the national anthem.

The people in front of the Imperial Palace cried out: "What a wonderful blessing it is that Tenno himself can call on us and we can hear his own voice in person. We are thoroughly satisfied in such a great sacrifice." Part of the crowd broke into a storage shed and got drunk on stocks of rice wine, or on *suri* and *duburoku*, illegal, home-made brews. Others burst into tears; many beat the ground in despair with their burned fists. The majority simply slipped away silently, resigned to their fate. Without a word of protest, without firing

---

[1]  By 1942, the American Navy had cracked the Japanese Code. Tokyo's plans for the Battle of Midway were studied in advance by the U.S. Navy. So, in June 1942, when a huge Japanese task force set off, it steamed straight into the gray jaws of a steel trap set by Admiral Nimitz. The Japanese lost four big aircraft carriers and the best of its Fleet Air Arm. Never again was Japan able to wrest the naval initiative. But the Japanese public was never given any inkling of these reverses; neither this nor the defeats at Bougainville, the Solomon Islands, and Okinawa were mentioned. Most Japanese were steadfast in their belief that continued efforts and sacrifices would lead to ultimate victory.

another shot, the war was ended, providing the greatest example of discipline, history has ever witnessed.[2]

Fr. Arrupe argued that it was *not* the atomic bombs that brought about the end of the war:

> The final cause of the end of the war was not the atomic bomb but the order of the Japanese Emperor demanding that his people surrender unconditionally, and their blind obedience to their *Teno Heika* (Emperor). It is not easy for one who does not understand the real situation and the true spirit of the *Yamato damishi* (Japanese spirit) to grasp the significance of the order. The Japanese would not have surrendered without it; they would have fought even hand-to-hand combat to defend their beloved *Yamato* from profanation by the enemy.
>
> The history of Japan underwent a complete turn-around at the end of the war. It was a change of course produced by a force entirely different from that which Oppenheimer or Truman applied against Japan … What would have happened had there been a move to try the Emperor as a war criminal (as in reality, some had thought of doing)? No collective force would have been able to change the course of a history that began with Amatersau and continued for 2,700 years, manifesting an uninterrupted series of dynasties and emperors. Only the voice of the same *Kami* (Emperor) could provide the termination of the story and be accepted without discussion or rebellion by his *Ko* (children).[3]

For everyone at the Novitiate, the day was one of great celebration. Not only because the war had ended. It was the Feast of the Assump-

---

2   It is ironic that this day, August 15, the day of surrender, was traditionally revered as a day of great victory. In 1281, the great Mogul emperor, Kublai Khan, attacked Japan with a huge invasion fleet. But on August 15, a typhoon struck Hakata Bay off Kyushu Island, crushing the Mongol boats together or piling them like matchwood on the northern peninsula. For the Japanese, that wind was no ordinary wind; it was' *kamikaze*,' a *divine* wind … But on *this* August 15, suddenly the Japanese people had to make a complete about-face and surrender unconditionally. And this they did—because the Emperor had commanded it.

3   Pedro Arrupe, S.J., *Recollections and Reflections*, pp. 55–57.

tion of Our Lady. And it was the anniversary of the first Jesuit mission-ary setting foot on Japanese soil — St. Francis Xavier, the former Basque aristocrat, who landed on Kagoshima, August 15, 1549. On January 1, 1946, the most important feast of the Japanese—on that day, the birthdays of all the subjects of the empire are celebrated—the Emperor again ordered that all his subjects listen to him on their radios. In a message transmitted from the Imperial Palace in Tokyo, the Emperor acknowledged that the secular belief in his divinity was false; he was not divine, but a man like any other. This dogma of faith, so basic to their national ideology, was dashed to pieces. For the Japanese, the Emperor was their Kano, their God and therefore invin-cible. Then suddenly had come the unconditional surrender and the Emperor declaring: *"I am not God."*

This total material and spiritual rupture was a devastating third bomb, a moral bomb, much more terrible that the two that had exploded over the skies of Japan ... In his *Recollections*, Fr. Arrupe wrote:

> Thus we will understand that the first consequence of the uncon-ditional surrender and the denial of the Emperor's divinity was a disorientation whose magnitude can only be measured by the unusual catastrophe that occasioned it. It was a total disorienta-tion because, with one breath, the light that illuminated the Japanese for 2600 years had been extinguished; suddenly all around them was darkness. And as if the surrender were not enough, the military totalitarianism to which they had been accustomed fell with the same blow, leaving the Japanese to think for themselves for the first time in history.[4]

The surrender ceremonies took place on the U.S. battleship Missouri on September 2, 1945. The American Occupation troops moved into Hiro-shima on October 10. How would the Japanese react at the arrival of executioners responsible for the slaughter in Hiroshima and Nagasaki? As Fr. Arrupe states: "There was an air of expectancy much like that of two *Sumotori* (Judo opponents) who watch carefully every movement of the adversary, even the most insignificant, before attacking."[5]

---

[4]    *Ibid.*, p. 43.
[5]    *Ibid.*, p. 58.

General Douglas MacArthur, looking even more imperial than the Emperor, set up his *Dai-ichi* or headquarters, in Tokyo. He was to be assisted in the work of governance by the Liberal Democratic Party, a party that supported American policies.

At first, the Japanese believed they would be treated badly by the American Occupation troops. But when they saw the GIs come down from their jeeps and play with their children, giving them sweets and chewing gum and clothing, their hatred relented. The armies of occupation, for their part, behaved honorably. The mutual collaboration was most commendable: absolute submission on the part of the Japanese on one hand and on the other, generosity and friendship on the part of the victors. American Shogun MacArthur was masterminding a military occupation which will go down as one of the most peaceful in history, the friendship between the General and the Emperor being a big factor in it. MacArthur's reforms, designed to root democracy deep into Japanese life, so as to make return to militarism impossible and to restore a shattered economy, won the Japanese people's support.

# 9 THE POSTWAR YEARS: 1945–1953

THE CALL FOR Fr. Arrupe to continue medical service to the people of Hiroshima went on during the year following the war's end. People, young and old, came to ask his help. Many were suffering from radiation sickness. Immediate symptoms like severe sore throat, hair loss, widespread rash, fever, all could be followed by sudden death. Fr. Arrupe determined that blood transfusions might save lives.

Mr. Taminoto, the Methodist minister who had worked so heroically with the Jesuits to rescue some of their own number and many of the other victims in the city succumbed to this sickness. Fr. Kleinsorge became quite ill but survived.

On September 17, 1945, the poor island-city of Hiroshima suffered a second major catastrophe. A hurricane struck with torrential rain and an 80 mph. wind. Half of the city's bridges that had survived the atomic blast were destroyed. The city's streets were flooded. An old Amy hospital being used by a team of medical experts from Kyoto Imperial University to study radiation sickness suddenly slid down the mountain where it was located, into the Inland Sea, drowning everyone in it, investigators and patients alike.

As time went on, Hiroshima's food supplies began to run low; the city saw the incidence of robberies, rapes, and murders escalate as well the practice of prostitution.

More positively, a group of twenty young medical students who were meeting with Arrupe formed a strong bond with him and eventually asked to be baptized. And among the returning Japanese service personnel were sixteen young men who entered the Novitiate in Nagatsuka and began their life as Jesuits under the direction of Fr. Arrupe. These would later become Jesuit University Presidents, Jesuit High School Principals and the Japanese Province Provincial.

During these years, Arrupe translated four books into Japanese, two spiritual classics and two books about Marxism. In 1950, he was elected to participate in a meeting with the Jesuit General in Rome and there he was directed to go around the world telling about his experience of the atomic bomb and also raising money for the Jesuit works in Japan. He was relieved of his post as Director of Novices.

# 10 PROVINCIAL OF THE JESUITS IN JAPAN: 1954–1965

O N MARCH 23, 1954, Fr. Arrupe was made Provincial of the 200 Jesuits working in Japan, men from 29 countries. The country and the Jesuits were still struggling to find enough to eat.

As Provincial, Arrupe continued to work extremely hard, retiring at midnight and getting up each morning at 4 a.m. He was quite engaging and loving toward the men he governed. One Spanish Jesuit said of him that he was an "optimist at all costs and perhaps he believed in people too much." Fr. Yamamuto, a Japanese Jesuit, described him as a "leader of great charism rather than an administrator. He needed to be surrounded by realists who would make his ideals work."

In 1957 and again in 1961, he made a six-month trip around the world, raising money for the Japanese mission and speaking about the terrible horror of the atomic bomb. He was a born speaker. His lectures were given with great enthusiasm and a sense of humor, full of anecdotes.

In 1958, he visited Nagasaki, now rebuilt from the ruins of the atomic bomb drop on August 9 of 1945. Nagasaki is the city where, in 1597, three Jesuit priests and six Franciscan priests and fifteen native Japanese converts were crucified, and lanced to death as they were hanging on their crosses. During his visit to Nagasaki, where Arrupe was intending to found a parish and build a school, he was asked by the Jesuit Archbishop of that place also to build a monument to honor the martyrs, and a museum, too.

In 1958, the Japanese Jesuit Province was experiencing unprecedented growth. A University of Music was founded at Hiroshima. Sophia, the Jesuit university in Tokyo, was expanded to include schools of Law, Physics, Engineering, and a Department of Spanish with the best linguistics laboratory in the world. Its student enrollment tripled from the 1500 students it had seen enrolled in 1945. New churches were built in Yamaguchi and Kobe, and a new retreat house was built.

During this time, Arrupe wrote eight books in Japanese, including a life of St. Francis Xavier and a five-volume commentary on the Spiritual Exercises of St. Ignatius Loyola. He also wrote (in Spanish) about Japan and his experience of the atomic bomb. He also maintained correspondence and significant friendships with the King and Queen of Belgium, Prince Juan Carlos and Princess Sophia of Spain, the Presidents of Argentina, Peru, and Germany, ... Popes Pius XII and John XXIII, and General Franco.

On June 10, 1962, the Feast of Pentecost in that year, a monument to peace was consecrated in Nagasaki. Because of a lack of funds, the planned Cathedral and museum would not be completed until later.

1962 would be a monumental year for the Catholic Church. For on June 10, Pope John XXIII convoked the Second Vatican Council.

One of the major issues which that Council would deliberate was that of modern warfare. Was war ever justified and was the use of the nuclear bomb ever justified? The Council declared:

> Any act of war aimed indiscriminately at the destruction of entire cities or of extensive areas along with their populations is a crime against God and man himself. It merits unequivocal and unhesitating condemnation.[1]

During the Second Vatican Council, Pope John XXII died and Cardinal Giovanni Montini, Pope Paul VI, assumed the leadership of the Catholic Church. Fr. Arrupe continued as Japanese Provincial. He watched as Japan changed greatly. The new problem for Japan was not shortages but overabundance. Japan had become the most advanced nation economically and technologically in the East; it had industriously incorporated Western ideologies, and the product of this hybrid was a skepticism and relativism that invaded everything. It required, therefore, a great effort on the part of the Jesuits to navigate this new mix of Western materialism and Japanese sensitivity and natural reserve so as to be able to show the wonder of the message of Jesus.

---

[1]   Vatican II, The Pastoral Constitution on the Church in the Modern World *Gaudium et Spes*, 80.

During this period of Arrupe's time as Provincial, he came under criticism from a group of German Jesuits in Japan who felt that he was moving too fast with his new ideas. They asked for someone to be sent by the Roman Jesuit central office to evaluate Arrupe's leadership. Fr. George Kester, S.J., who had been Provincial of the Jesuits in Indonesia, was sent to Japan to do an evaluation. Kester had been on this assignment for about a year when the Jesuit General John Baptist Janssens, S.J. died on October 5, 1964.

A General Council of the Jesuits was called and began on May 7, 1965; 265 Jesuits, representing the Order's 36,000 members, from 90 counties, attended. Their main mission was to choose a new General.[2]

Because the General Congregation is to be attended by all the Jesuit Provincials as well as by one or two other delegates from each Province —depending on the size of a Province—, Fr. Arrupe, as Japanese Provincial, attended and on the third ballot, he was chosen to become the twenty-eighth General of the Jesuit Order.

Vatican Radio spoke of him as "an idealist and an able administrator." Asked by a journalist, "How will you fight atheism?" Arrupe replied with a smile:

> We won't be fighting anyone or anything. Our tactic is not fighting but dialogue, mutual respect, learning to listen, trying to understand the obstacles that keep people from the knowledge of God. We must treat those who disagree with us with the same gentleness that the Japanese treat the cherry flower.

Fr. Arrupe moved into the Father General's residence in the Jesuit Curia building, about 100 paces from the Vatican. Below his room were the fifteen offices and secretariats, manned by 120 Jesuits of all colors and nationalities, all experts in their specialist fields.

On one of his first days at the office of the General, Arrupe found a file on his desk. It was a report—on him!—prepared by Fr. Kester in Japan! "Poor Fr. Kester!" the new Jesuit General remarked with a smile.

---

[2]    In the Jesuit tradition, this process is to occur without any politicking, and should anyone attempt to win votes, he is to be removed from consideration and from the congregation itself.

# 11 Arrupe's Work as General: 1965–1973

**W**HEN THE JESUIT order was begun under the leadership of St. Ignatius Loyola and its other original founders, it was determined that the focus and the spirit of the group would be missionary. Unlike other conventual religious orders like the Benedictines, in order to promote maximum mobility, the Jesuits' legislative congregations would be rare; and the leader chosen to direct them as their "General" would be chosen to hold that position for life.

So, over its 410 year history, the Jesuits had held only thirty-one "General Congregations" and had seen only twenty-seven General Superiors. Fr. Arrupe was the twenty-eighth Jesuit General. At the thirty-first General Congregation, at which he was elected, it was decreed that the General, who by Jesuit law was expected to govern until his death, but could be permitted to resign if poor health impaired his ability to govern; in this case, with the approval of his "General Assistants" and the vote of all the Jesuit Provincials, a General Congregation would be convoked and a new General would be elected.

Fr. Arrupe, as it turned out, would govern the Jesuits for 18 years, until a very serious stroke caused him to resign. On October, 6, 1981, one of his Assistants, Fr. Dezza, S.J. took over as 'temporary General" until a General Congregation could be convoked on February, 1982, the thirty-third General Congregation in Jesuit history, which chose Fr. Peter Hans Kolvenbach, S.J. to succeed Fr. Arrupe. Fr. Kovenbach become the twenty-ninth General of the Jesuit order. [There had been a thirty-second General Congregation held in 1973–74, during the middle of Fr. Arrupe's Generalate.]

What follows now is a summary of the major goals and achievements of Fr. Arrupe's Generalate as well as some of its struggles and most engaging events.

It will help understanding of this man's style and his genius to know that he now rose at 4 a.m., then prayed in the chapel near his bedroom from 4:15 to 6 a.m., celebrated Eucharist at 6 a.m., had breakfast at 7:30, briefly looked at the headlines of the newspapers, did personal study, mostly of theology from 7:45-9 a.m., was briefed on matters of importance by his Secretary General at 9 a.m. (but once a week met at that time, 9 a.m., with his four General Assistants); between 9:30 and 12:30 p.m., he wrote letters, had visitors, prepared talks; at 12:30 p.m. had prayers with the community and at 1 p.m. dinner followed by some conversation and brief TV; then returned to work in the mid-afternoon and with time out for supper, continued to work until midnight. It also helps to know that Fr. Arrupe had grown to be fluent in 7 languages.[1]

On September 27, 1965, Fr. Arrupe was asked to give a talk at Vatican Council II to the assembly of 2200 Council members about "The Church and Modern Times." He spoke especially about atheism: "The cure of this problem is a Christian society; in a world animated by a Christian spirit, people will become religious."

On December 19, 1965, the General began an exhausting tour of the Middle East and Africa. Beirut, Cairo, Addis Ababa, Damascus, Baghdad; then all the missions in north and central Africa—Zambia, Rhodesia, the Congo, Cameroon, Chad, and then Tripoli.

In 1966, Arrupe paid a visit to France where there was no lack of Jesuits. On April, 1966, he traveled with Fr. Vincent O'Keefe to the United States, and gave a talk at Fordham University about "human rights, freedom and the dignity of the human person."

On December 12, 1966, the Feast of the Virgin of Guadalupe, he sent a letter to the Latin-American Jesuits on the subject of social justice. Were their activities directed enough towards the service of the poor? Certain of their schools were geared to the wealthy. Should these be closed or at least made available to the poor?

In 1967, Arrupe travelled to India and Sri Lanka where there were 1,830 Jesuits, of whom 1,780 were natives of the sub-continent. He traveled there for three months, urging the Jesuits there to educate

---

[1] It would almost certainly *be wrong* and a *serious mistake* for most of us to try *to work as long and to sleep as little* as Fr. Arrupe.

the people for the agricultural and industrial revolutions taking place in those countries.

In April, 1967, he set off for Alaska, Canada, and the United States. In the United States, on November 1, 1967, Fr. Arrupe wrote a letter to the U.S. Jesuits about the racial crisis in the U.S. and about racial segregation, not only of Blacks but also of Hispanics, Native Americans, and immigrants. The Jesuits must concentrate, he said, on the minorities, work in Black areas, promote integration in their schools, and when appropriate, locate their own residences in Black neighborhoods.[2]

In 1967, Arrupe went into a cinema in Bogota to see the film Hiroshima. He describes the inner turmoil this brought him:

> In an hour and a half I saw before me on the screen, the horror and tragedy I had lived during several months. My vision became clouded with tears and I could stand it no longer; I left my seat and walked out. It was too much for me! What I had experienced in Hiroshima in six months throughout the reality of the day-by-day, minute-by-minute events was too massive a dose of reality to be relived in a mere hour. Humiliating contradiction! What I withstood in all its terrible reality overcame me completely in the unreality of a celluloid film. My nerves, which I thought were made of iron, were shattered by that emotional onslaught.

In 1967, Fr. Arrupe was elected President of the Union of Superiors General of all religious Orders. He would be re-elected five times to this leadership position until 1981, the year of his resignation.

In April of 1968, together with Pope Paul VI, in his role as President of the Union of Superiors General, Fr. Arrupe attended the Conference of Bishops of Latin America. There was Arrupe's good friend, Bishop Dom Helder Camara, known for his open denunciation of the flagrant injustice, racial discrimination, and ideology of violence that were ravaging Latin America. The Pope encouraged Dom Helder to begin a campaign of active non-violence in the style of Martin Luther King.[3]

---

[2] Below, at the end of this summary of his work, you will be invited to discuss issues related to racism.

[3] It is not surprising that one day when the smiling Bishop in his frayed cassock returned home, he found it had been raided and his secretary assassinated.

So, Fr. Arrupe, who had met with the Provincials of Latin America for a week of study and reflection, sent a letter to all the Jesuits of Latin America, urging them, despite the threats of violence, to continue to preach the Gospel to the poor, to defend the weak and the dispossessed, to fight for a more just society, with equal rights for everyone, and to liberate the people from servitude and oppression. "We cannot remain silent, in certain countries before regimes which constitute, without any doubt, a sort of institutionalized violence." To this letter, there was an inevitable reaction and denunciation from some of the privileged classes.

On August 15, 1968, shortly after the publication of the Pope's encyclical *Humanae Vitae*, which condemned use of contraceptives and which was opposed by some Jesuits, Fr. Arrupe wrote to all Jesuits asking for filial obedience. He pointed out that to obey was not to stop thinking and that Jesuits had to discover the sense of this papal teaching while they also collaborated with the centers of investigation run by the human sciences.

In April, 1969, he made a trip to the Far East, and also visited Czechoslovakia and Poland. In Poland, he had a meeting with the future John Paul II.

In January 1970, he visited the Jesuits in England and Scotland. There he made a moving informal address praising the mothers of Jesuits who have given up their sons to serve the Church as Jesuit priests and brothers.

In May and again in December of 1970, he visited for the first time since he began his work as Jesuit General, his native homeland, Spain. During this time, He had to deal with severe problems of disunity among the Jesuits there. He visited 21 cities and his visits and loving manner brought peace and renewed spirit to the seven Jesuit Provinces of Spain. During that time, he visited with General Franco, the Spanish dictator, and pleaded with him for an end to police brutality and torture.

In March of 1971, Arrupe returned to Japan, and then to eight other nations of the Far East—Thailand, Taiwan, Indonesia, Hong Kong, Australia, Korea, Oceania, and South Vietnam—where Jesuits were on mission. In India in April of 1971, he addressed 300 Jesuits from India and Sri Lanka about the way Jesuits should address the secular-ized spirit which had taken over their countries: "We [Jesuits] must count on a solidly built interior life [of prayer]."[4]

From April 30 to May 10 of 1971, Fr. Arrupe was in the United States to participate in a meeting of the Northern American Provincials at Los Gatos, In California. In a paper entitled "The Social Commitment of the Society of Jesus," he treated the extent to which Jesuits should and should not get involved in politics: "The priest should not encroach especially in the political sphere — so closely bound to the exercise of political power—, ...on a domain proper to lay-persons, to whom in this area belongs the last decision. The principal service a Jesuit can render here, and particularly in the political sphere, is not to take the place of the lay-persons in a role proper to them, but rather in dialogue with lay persons, to help them to take cognizance of and to embrace the right ethical elements involved in their decisions."

From the United States, Fr. Arrupe went on to Panama, and to Quito and Guayaquil in Ecuador. In Quito, walking down the main city thoroughfare, Fr. Arrupe was accosted by a 'street lad' who took his arm and led him to a high chair, pleading that he should have his shoes cleaned and polished. The boy proudly displayed his 'certificate of the working lad.' "Oh, I have one too," said Arrupe, "it is one of my prized possessions. It could of course be revoked for bad behavior, or for swearing in the streets ... You don't believe me?" With that, Father Arrupe took off his jacket, seated the young lad on the high chair and polished his shoes!

Arrupe later wrote of his experience of saying Mass for people in a terrible Latin-American slum:

> After the Mass, one old woman said, "Thank you for giving the greatest treasure we lacked, the holy Mass." One young man said openly, "Señor Padre, you should know that we are very thankful since these [Jesuit] priests here have taught us how to

---

4    Below, at the end of this review of Arrupe's life, you will be asked to reflect on the role which prayer should assume in the life of one who wishes to become a person 'for others'.

love our enemies. One week ago, I had prepared a knife to kill a comrade whom I hated much, but after I heard the priest explain the Gospel, I went and bought ice-cream and gave it to my enemy."

Also, then, a big fellow whose fearful looks could have inspired fear, told me: "Come to my house, I have something to honor you." I remained uncertain, not knowing whether I should accept or not, but the priest who was accompanying me, said: "Go with him, Father; the people are very good." I went to his house that was a half-falling shack. He made me sit down on a rickety chair. From where I was seated, the sun could be seen as it was setting. The fellow said to me: "Señor, see how beautiful it is!" And we remained silent for some minutes. The sun disappeared. The man added: "I did not know how to thank you for all that you have done for us. I have nothing to give you, but I thought you would like to see this sunset. It pleased you, didn't it. Good evening!" He then gave me his hand.

As I was leaving I thought: "I have met very few hearts that are so kind" … I was about to leave that street when a small woman very poorly dressed came up. She kissed my hand, looked at me and said to me with words full of emotion: "Father, pray for me and for my children. I was at that beautiful Mass which you celebrated. I am running home. But I have nothing to give my nine children. Pray to the Lord for me. He must help us." And she disappeared almost running in the direction of her house.

From Ecuador, Fr. Arrupe went to Lima Peru, where 10,000 homeless people had occupied the Jesuit school. Monsignor Bambaren, the Jesuit auxiliary bishop of Lima, sided with the occupiers and was arrested. Three days later, the Minister of the Interior resigned and the government offered new land to the occupying poor.

From Lima, Arrupe went to Rio de Janeiro to attend a meeting of the Jesuit Provincials of Latin America and discuss with them "the theology of liberation," and then August 16–20, 1971, onto Dublin to give an address to the Fourth International Congress of Jesuit Ecumenists. August 27 to September 1 of that year, he visited Russia and met Nikodim, the Metropolitan of Leningrad and also met the Patriarch of the Russian Orthodox Church. During that same month, he traveled to Manila in the Philippines, where he gave an address to representatives of Christian Churches about ecumenical dialogue. Returning in December of that year to Rome, he wrote to the Jesuits of Mexico involved in education that they should work hard in their schools to promote justice and compassion for the poor.

March of 1972, Arrupe was in Duala, in the Cameroons, where he gave an address to the Provincials of Africa that they should urge their men

> prudently and lovingly, through dialogue and collaboration with the followers of other religions, and in witness of Christian faith and life, [to] acknowledge, preserve and promote the spiritual and moral goods found among these men, as well as the values in their society and culture, ... and oppose the hectic pursuit of pleasure and of an imported pseudo-culture.

In a talk published in *America* magazine on September, 1972, Fr. Arrupe spoke about the goal of Jesuit education:

> Our students are not to see themselves as isolated individuals learning how to elbow their way through hostile masses to positions of power and prestige. Rather. let them discover in ways they can never forget that they are brothers [and sisters] in a planetary village, fellow pilgrims on spaceship earth. Perhaps, in the past, we stressed individual achievements too much. The 'new humanism' should place a counter-stress on the more social values: sensitivity to human need; concern for the poor, the oppressed, the marginalized—not so much as object of charity but as subjects of rights, as equals who must be helped to help themselves.

In this same vein, on July 31, 1973, Arrupe again spoke forcefully about the goal of Jesuit education, this time, to an International Congress of Jesuit Alumni, held in Valencia, Spain, to 700 alumni/ae of Jesuit schools. The theme of his talk was the last [Spanish] Bishops synod, which had highlighted the role of justice in the lives of Catholic believers. Arrupe touched on the consumerist, permissive, and selfish society in which most of his listeners lived. He expressed the need for greater simplicity of life, for attachment to fewer belongings, for a society in favor of the weaker. He spoke of "Men for Others." The speech became famous in this slogan, which described the purpose and goal of Jesuit education. He later broadened the formula to "Men and Women for Others" ... His speech did not go down well with some of his audience and was followed by a number of resignations from the Congress of Jesuit Alumni. However, this speech was to become famous, and Cardinal Villot, the Secretary of State at the Vatican, wrote and thanked Arrupe for his "evangelical message."

As you hear of Fr. Arrupe's talks both to Jesuits and to the leaders and graduates of Jesuit schools in Spain, in Latin America, and the U.S., about the right goal of Jesuit schools, namely, to fashion "men and women for others," and to help students to see that greed and the desire for power can be enemies of the true mission of those schools, notice that some of his hearers did not like what Arrupe said!

# 12 THE 32ND GENERAL CONGREGATION

ON SEPTEMBER 8, 1973, Fr. Arrupe called a meeting of a General Congregation, the thirty-second, in the history of the Jesuit order. Its purpose was to discuss the type of work the Order should be doing in a time of rapid change. Much research had gone into preparation for this gathering, starting in 1970. The Congregation officially began in December, 1974. On December 29, Fr. Arrupe gave a talk to the assembled Congregation on the role of "Simplicity of Life in the Mission of Jesuits." He described the courage, humility and discipline needed to go to a foreign country and live there as a poor person, learning the language of the country and often being looked down upon as one learned a new language and aimed to show allegiance to the forgotten and outcast of that society. This, he seemed to imply, should be the spirit of all Jesuits.

A major issue that Fr. Arrupe wished to take up, and which was the first major item on the Congregation's agenda was the question of whether all Jesuits—brothers and priests—might take the exact same vows and have the same authority in the order. Pope Paul VI did not want such a change to be considered for fear both that it would damage the vision of the Jesuits that had been shaped by its founder, St. Ignatius, and for fear that it would lead to significant problems in the missionary functioning of the order. [All Jesuits take the three vows of poverty, chastity and obedience. But only some of the priests, those deemed more suited for leadership, also take a vow of special obedience to the Pope in matters of mission.] In obedience to Pope Paul VI's wish, this topic was removed from discussion.

What was then discussed was the place that justice must have in the service of the Catholic faith. Arrupe's constant concern for the poor, the marginalized, the dispossessed, and the spirit of concern and admiration for the 20 Jesuits martyred in the Third World for their defense of the rights of the poor, motivated the 236 delegates present to pass legislation which articulated in its fourth decree, the mandate that *"the promotion of justice was to be an essential factor in every Jesuit effort to promote the Catholic Christian faith."* This decree stated that the problem of justice must be attacked not only on a social plane but at its root—namely, those attitudes and tendencies that generate injustice and oppression—greed, materialism, the desire for power, and so forth.

The thirty-second General Congregation and this fourth decree have inspired and directed all the works of the Jesuit order and the legislation of each of the three congregations that have followed.

On March 7, 1975, Pope Paul VI met with Fr. Arrupe and his four General Assistants to express his appreciation of the Order. As a symbol of his gratitude, he gave Fr. Arrupe a crucifix that had once belonged to the saintly Jesuit and cardinal, Robert Bellarmine. Arrupe was quite moved by this gesture.

# 13 ARRUPE'S FINAL WORK AS GENERAL

AFTER THE CONCLUSION of the General Congregation, Fr. Arrupe returned to his work. One American Jesuit, realizing the intense pace at which he worked, invited him to go to a pizzeria with him. "But everyone will recognize me," Arrupe pointed out. "Then put on a wig." "But what shall I put on my nose?" Arrupe joked.

In August, 1975, Fr. Arrupe addressed a meeting in Rome of 70 Jesuit Rectors and Presidents of Universities and Colleges from all over the world. He sounded a call for 'prophets' –

> for persons who speak God's message, not only when it is willingly accepted but also when it is seen as a "hard saying," painful to the all-too-human ways of viewing what God expects of man in history. Our teaching will be directed to forming the new human person, an integrated personality, instead of the customary maimed, one dimensional products of our cultural technology ... We shall build up *Men and Women for Others*, whose ideal is that of service, who enrich their own personalities for the enrichments of others; whose horizons stretch out to their brothers and sisters across the farthest national and international frontiers ... Men and women who are in continual contact with the world of science without losing touch with the world of the Spirit.

The following August, 1976, Fr. Arrupe was invited to give two talks in Philadelphia, to the International Eucharistic Congress, which was holding "the International Symposium on Hunger." In his talks, he called **"arms spending intolerable,"** and asked his hearers to do all they can to help put an end to famine and poverty.

The letter which he wrote and sent to all Jesuits on November 1, 1976, The Feast of All Saints, about *"the Integration of a Jesuit's Spiritual Life and His Missionary Work"* was one of his best documents and would have a profound impact on the life of many Jesuits.

In November, 1976, Arrupe was asked to speak at a conference in Frankfurt, West Germany, about the responsibility of Europeans in the fields of faith and justice toward the people of the Third World:

> After the Eucharistic Congress in Philadelphia, I set out for Honduras, Guatemala, and Venezuela. I visited some of my fellow Jesuits who live in dilapidated hovels among the poor, and I celebrated the Eucharist in makeshift churches in the slums where I distributed the Bread of Life to starving marginalized people. After the Mass, many came up to me, among them the mother of nine children. I shall never forget her face, marked by hunger and suffering. She said to me: "Father General, I have nothing left to give my children. Pray for me, that God may send us some bread." In that moment, I understood more clearly than ever before that I had not exaggerated in Philadelphia or at any other place where I had talked about hunger in the world. Encounter with starving persons has been decisive for me. I have met them not only individually, but also in groups, in masses, in entire countries ...

On January 15, 1977, Fr. Arrupe celebrated the golden anniversary of his becoming a Jesuit at a Mass at the Church of the Gesù in Rome. There he spoke of *three models* and patrons that had inspired his life:

1. *Abraham*, who responded promptly to God's call, to go forth from his own land, to take up his abode elsewhere in a place unknown to him. His were my thoughts as I decided to enter the Jesuits, to set out to work in Japan, and to take up the duty of being General of the Jesuit Order.

2. *St. Paul*, who helped me to weather difficulties, misunderstandings and obstacles. "There is nothing I cannot master with the help of the One who gives me strength." (Philippians 4:13) "With God on our side, who can be against us?" (Romans 8:13)

3. *St. Francis Xavier*, who understood brilliantly the value of the cross and suffering, and whose real source of energy was trust in God.

In March 1977, Fr. Rutillo Grande, S.J. was murdered in El Salvador. He had spoken out for the poor of that country and on behalf of peasant organizations. He was one of five Jesuits doing such work in Central America, Brazil, and Zimbabwe who were killed during 1976 and 1977. Fr. Arrupe wrote to all Jesuits praising the courage of these men. Then between 1978 and 1981, 20 more Jesuits were also to give their lives defending the faith and fighting non-violently for justice to the poor and downtrodden.

In October of 1977, on the Feast of the Jesuits martyred in North America as they worked among the Native Americans in 1637, Arrupe wrote a letter to all Jesuits asking for their availability to go wherever they might be needed throughout the world even to the most difficult locations.

Asked to speak at a meeting of religious 'superiors' from North and South America held in Montreal, Canada, on November 21, 1977, he blasted the spirit of consumerism which moved people to aim only at piling up wealth with no care for the poor:

> Our world is threatened by two ghosts: poverty and war. By 2000 A.D., the rich will have grown richer, the poor, poorer. The numerical difference between rich and poor and the qualitative difference between their standards of living will have become gigantic. How long can this go on?! ...The greatest service that religious priests, religious brothers and sisters can offer to humankind is to give irrefutable witness against such selfish consumerism by a life that is austere and frugal.

On August 6, 1978, Pope Paul VI died. On October 16, Cardinal Karol Wojtyła, became the first Pope to come from Poland. He took the name John Paul II.

Arrupe's fame and leadership had grown to such an extent that there were fears for this life. The Red Brigade (in Italy) had recently kidnapped the Italian politician Aldo Moro. It was believed that Arrupe was next on the list of kidnap or assassination. Arrupe reminded his colleagues, *"Remember, don't give them one lira (penny) for me."* One of his General Assistants would arrange when Arrupe had to travel that the Italian police would supply an escort.

On October 31, 1978, he gave a talk about the Jesuit Brothers and their great importance in the work of the Jesuit order. It was the feast day of a sainted Jesuit Brother named Alphonsus Rodriguez.

In February of 1979, Fr. Arrupe attended a meeting of the Third Conference of Latin American Bishops held in Puebla, Mexico. At a press conference there, he was told that the Jesuits were blamed for the troubles in El Salvador. He replied:

> The Jesuits in El Salvador are working for justice and are doing a good job. When in [last] July, they were threatened that if they didn't leave, they would be killed, I told them to stay. The Jesuit Order will not be moved by threats. (Applause) ...Opponents have killed seven of our men, three in Rhodesia, four in Beirut; and [we Jesuits] have been thrown out of Iraq. [We] are not frightened.[1]

Ten years later, in 1989, six Jesuit professors working at the University of Central America in El Salvador, along with their rectory housekeeper and her daughter, would be shot to death in their rectory yard by members of the Salvadoran army.

At a gathering of 42 National Federations of "Christian Life Communities,"[2] Arrupe was asked, "How do you think a member of the CLC should react to institutionalized violence?" He replied:

> With a non-violent resistance—hunger strikes, public denunciations, political action, discussions, meetings and demonstrations. All these are acceptable; *violence, no!* ...Violence is anti- evangelical [contrary to Jesus' gospel teachings]; and so no Catholic should engage in it.

On January 8, 1980, Arrupe began a trip to the East, to India, Nepal, and Thailand. In India, he visited de Nobili College, Pune, the largest house of formation for Jesuits in the world. He was greeted with great enthusiasm by the Jesuit seminarians. On his return from this trip, he learned the sad news that his very dear sister Maria, a nun, had died

---

1    At this conference, Arrupe was the only person accompanied by bodyguards.
2    CLC is a Jesuit spiritual organization for lay persons which is very popular in many countries, but perhaps less so, in the U.S..

after a long life of suffering. Unfortunately, he could not make the journey to attend her funeral.

On February 9 and 10 of 1980, 13 Jesuits living as 'worker-priests' in 6 different European countries came to see Fr. Arrupe in Rome. They had been given permission to live and to labor as the very poor workers in each of their own countries did, so as to build a bridge with them and to enable these very poor workers to see that the Catholic Church understood them and their very difficult life. Arrupe, commending these 13 Jesuits for their humility and care, urged them also to be sure to keep up their own spiritual life of prayer and to offer the Eucharist daily, as well as to maintain their openness to being missioned elsewhere if their Provincials chose to change their assignment.

In April of 1980, Arrupe, who was 73, feeling his strength diminishing, asked Pope John Paul II if he might begin the process of resigning and arranging for a new Jesuit General. The Pope asked him not to do so.

June 22, 1980, was a big day for the Jesuits. Pope John Paul II canonized the great Jesuit, Fr. Anchieta S.J., who together with his colleagues, had been largely responsible for the conversion of Brazil to Christianity.

A few days later, he met with his surviving two sisters, in Manresa, Spain, for the first time since the death of their sister Maria; then he went on to Lisbon, Portugal and back to Rome, to prepare for a long trip to India, Ceylon, Singapore, and Bangkok, Thailand. He was still hoping for another meeting with the Pope for he was feeling his health failing.

In August of 1980, Fr. Arrupe had made the eight days of prayer-retreat, which Jesuits are expected to make each year. He had asked Fr. Luis Gonzalez, Director of the Ignatian Center for Spirituality in Rome, to help lead him in his prayer. Fr. Gonzalez would later say, presumably having received from Fr. Arrupe permission to speak about the usually confidential matter of a directee's retreat, that Fr. Arrupe had experienced much consolation throughout the retreat, assurances of God's approval both for his labors and also for his intention to offer his resignation. However, on the seventh day of the retreat, the day on which Jesuit retreatants often pray over the suffering and death of Jesus on the cross, Fr. Arrupe felt desolation as he had never felt it before and experienced rebellion at the thought of his own suffering and humiliation. Next day, however, the last day of his retreat, he recovered his usual calm. This retreat experience was perhaps a premonition of what was soon to come soon in Fr. Arrupe's life.

On May 13, 1981, Arrupe was having a meeting with Jesuit Superiors from Africa, when suddenly a young Jesuit priest ran in, to announce that Pope John Paul II had been shot. As the Pope was being driven around St. Peter's Square, a man named Ali Agca had shot the Pope and he had been taken to Gemelli Hospital. The Pope would eventually recover from his serious wound, and Fr. Arrupe would visit him in Gemelli Hospital before Arrupe had to set out for the Philippines.

On July 25 of 1981, he set out for the Philippines for 12 days to celebrate the fourth centennial anniversary of the Jesuits' presence in those islands. In the Philippines he presided at 14 Mass celebrations, spoke to 26 different groups and at 26 more meetings. In a meeting at the Ateneo de Manila, there were 380 Jesuits and on July 31, the Feast of the Jesuit founder, St. Ignatius, at a banquet attended by 200 Jesuits and Archbishop Dominic Tang, who had spent 22 years in prison in China, Fr. Arrupe joined with the Basque Jesuits present to sing the Basque song *Boga Boga*. Arrupe, who had a great baritone voice, then sang a duet in Japanese with his close Jesuit friend, Bob Rush. The assembly then finished with the *Salve Regina*. Bishop Tang said of this celebration: "In 30 years, I have not enjoyed such a good experience!"

On August 5, 1981, Arrupe with two Jesuit assistants flew to Bangkok, Thailand. On the sixth day of his visit, he met with the Jesuits working in the appalling refugee camps in Thailand—desolate areas of land under guard, containing hundreds of thousands of Vietnamese, Laotians, and Cambodians, with no country and no future. The Jesuits lived with them in their solitude and their poverty. The Jesuits expressed freely to Arrupe their problems, including their difficult relations with the local church. "Please don't give up," he exhorted them. "Pray. We are on the front line of a new kind of mission for our Order. We need to be enlightened by the Holy Spirit."

On Christmas Eve of 1979, almost two years earlier, on hearing about the plight of the boat people and others fleeing from persecution in various countries of Southeast Asia, Africa and Central America, Arrupe and his staff had gathered food, medicine and money, and had created an organization called Jesuit Refugee Services [JRS] to aid refugees throughout the world. This would become one of Fr. Arrupe's greatest legacies to the Jesuit order.

# 14 The Cross

RETURNING FROM THAILAND, on August 6, 1981, with Fr. Laurendreau and Fr. Rush, Fr. Arrupe boarded a plane for an eleven-hour flight back to Rome. Arrupe looked very tired. They arrived at the airport in Rome at 5:30 a.m. and made their way to the baggage collection area. There at the carousel, Fr. Arrupe reached down to pick up his suitcase. He remained stooped and could not pick up his suitcase nor straighten up. Fr. Rusk and Fr. Laurendeau managed to pull Arrupe's body erect. Together they got him to a waiting car. Arrupe began muttering totally unconnected and incomprehensible words. The voice that could move and inspire and sometimes disturb his hearers in seven languages was now silent. The voice of the 'voiceless' now had no voice. Fr. Arrupe had had a severe stroke!

Ft. Arrupe was taken to Gemelli Hospital where Pope John Paul II was still recovering from his gunshot wound. The Pope from within the Hospital would send him a telegram expressing his cordial sympathy. Fr. Arrupe would be taken subsequently to the Jesuit General's residence where he would be given intensive sessions of physical therapy and speech-therapy. He had the greatest difficult moving his right hand and speaking in complete sentences. He had forgotten names. He could still understand the languages he had always used but he could express himself only in Spanish and even this, poorly.

On October 3, Fr. O'Keefe, the 'First' General Assistant wrote a letter to all the Superiors of the Jesuit Order regarding the possibility of a General Congregation to appoint a new General to replace Fr. Arrupe. However, on October 6, the Pope wrote a letter declaring that another of the four General Assistants, Fr. Dezza, 80 years old, should assume leadership of the Order temporarily and that the convocation of a new General Congregation should be delayed.

On February 23, 1983, Fr. Dezza called all the Jesuit Provincials to a meeting in Rome and they met with Pope John Paul II on February 27 and he gave permission for the calling of a General Congregation to elect a new General to replace Fr. Arrupe. The thirty-third General Congregation of the Jesuit order would begin in September of 1983.

At that Congregation, on September 3, Fr. Dezza delivered a eulogy of Fr. Arrupe, speaking of his spirit of sacrifice and his holy resignation in the face of his stroke. Fr. Arrupe, who assisted by two nurses had entered the Hall, was given a thunderous ovation by the 220 Jesuits present. A Jesuit friend, Fr. Ignacio Iglesias, read the farewell speech which Fr. Arrupe had drafted with the help of his Assistants:

> How I wish I were in better condition for this meeting with you. As you can see, I cannot even address you directly. But my General Assistants have grasped what I want to say to everyone.
>
> More than ever, I now find myself in the hands of God. This is what I have wanted all my life, from my youth. And this is still the one thing I want. But now there is a difference; the initiative is entirely with God. It is indeed a profound spiritual experience to know and feel myself so totally in His hands...
>
> In [my] eighteen years [as General of the Society], my one ideal was to serve the Lord and His Church—with all my heart—from beginning to end ...

He went on to thank God for the graces that had been given during his Generalate, to thank his Assistants for all their help, to thank all of his brother Jesuits for their dedication. He also exhorted young Jesuits to prepare for the future with courage and generosity, and those "at the peak of their apostolic activity, to be careful not to burn themselves out," and the elderly like himself, to submit to God's will for them *now*. He spoke a special "thanks" and reminded the Jesuit priests and seminarians of how much they all owed to the Jesuit brothers. As the speech concluded, following a great ovation and a presentation of an inscribed photograph of Pope John Paul II, Fr. Arrupe stood up, kissed the photograph of the Pope, then the hand of Fr. Dezza ... *The era of Arrupe was over.* ...On the arm of his nurse, he crossed the hall to the longest and most emotional ovation ever for a General!

On September 13, the Congregation, on its first ballot, elected as the 29th General of the Jesuit Order, Peter Hans Kolvenbach, S.J., a

Dutch Jesuit who had served for many years as a missionary in the Near East, most of that time, in Lebanon.

For ten years more, Fr. Arrupe would continue living with his disabilities, with much discomfort and suffering. However, people coming to see him would find him so warm and loving. On February 5, 1991, the feast of the Japanese martyrs of Nagasaki, he died, at the age of 83. Pope John Paul II exalted Arrupe—his devotion and love of the Church, his acceptance of the Divine Will in his suffering. Fr. Kolvenbach spoke of his "radiant optimism," and of how he had always sought how best to adapt the guidelines of Vatican II to the new times. Fr. Jon Sobrino, S.J. a noted Jesuit theologian, said of Pedro Arrupe at his burial:

> Here lies a man so human; he had a heart larger than the world in which he lived. One cannot help but love him.

# 15 Pedro Arrupe's Legacy

F R. Arrupe's impact on the spirit of the Jesuit order and upon its ministries can hardly be measured. Jesuit schools and universities have taken to heart his call to promote in their students not only academic learning but also a deep moral dedication to justice and compassion. Forming "men and women for others" is the goal to which all Jesuit educational institutions now aspire. And in Jesuit parishes and retreat houses, this same aspiration motivates pastors, retreat house directors and their staffs.

Arrupe's vision will gain greater notoriety if his cause for canonization continues to gain ground and if the Jesuit Refugee Service, which he instituted, helps more and more refugees to be treated with compassion, to escape from violence, and to find a new home where their children will be safe.

As a conclusion to the story of Pedro Arrupe's life and as a step to further his holy legacy, you are invited now to ponder and hopefully to discuss how well you and your school embody the values and meet *five* concerns which Fr. Arrupe wanted to become part of the Jesuit tradition:

1. How well does your Jesuit school *promote education for justice?* What are the programs and practices at the school which contribute to that goal? Is there any area that needs improvement?

2. Fr. Arrupe often decried *the spirit of materialism and selfish consumerism*—the desire of *"more for me"* and even a selfish desire for power. The society in which we are living often advocates pursuit of sexual pleasure to the detriment of generous care for and dedicated service of others ... Do such desires ever find a place in your life or in the lives of your classmates? ... Should they? ... How are such desires resisted and how can they be overcome?

3. Fr. Arrupe underscored for Jesuits and for their associates the importance of *the practice of prayer.* Do you make time each day to pray? Hopefully, in this respect, you have been shown at your

school the value of the "consciousness examen." Do you use the "consciousness examen" each day to guide your use of time, your decisions and your choices? ... And the Eucharist ("Mass") , seen as a ritual commemorating Jesus' sacrifice on our behalf, a modeling of courage to inspire our generosity and dedication, can motivate Christians to give their lives in service to others ... Does this prayer-form as well as the consciousness examen help you and your classmates? Is there any reason why they don't?

4.   During the summer or on school holidays, has your Jesuit school sent any students to work with foreign immigrant refugees or oppressed U.S. populations, either at the border or on a Native ("Indian") reservation? ... Have any of your classes treated the Christian's duty to reach out to aid immigrant refugees and their families fleeing violence in their homelands?

5.   How well do you think your Jesuit school has implemented Fr. Arrupe's call to *fight racism*? Do you and you classmates show love and respect for all races at your school? Do the faculty and admin-istration? How much do we need to try to understand the culture of another race, a culture which may be different from our own? ...Do you think a discussion of racism should include discussion of appropriate guidelines for police officers, a discussion which balances (a) a real respect for those officers who carry out their duties bravely, fairly, and compassionately, (b) and an acknowl-edgement that some officers need to be called to account or fired for their racial attitudes, and some need better training and preparation for handling persons who are mentally sick?

Your reflection and discussion of these five issues will promote the great and noble legacy of Fr. Arrupe.

---

Dear reader, as you conclude this book, perhaps, *on whatever path God in your future may call YOU to walk*, you may want to take to take to heart the following thought composed by Fr. Joseph Whelan, S.J., an Assist-ant to Fr. Arrupe, as a legacy attributed with good reason to Fr. Arrupe:

*Pedro Arrupe's Legacy*

*Nothing is more practical than **finding God**,*
*that is, than...*
*FALLING IN LOVE.*
*In a quite absolute, final way, what you are in love with,*
*what seizes your imagination, will affect everything!*
*It will decide what gets you out of bed in the morning,*
*what you do in the evenings,*
*how you spend your weekends, what you read, who you know,*
*what breaks your heart,*
*and what amazes you with joy and gratitude!*
*Fall in love, stay in love!*
*And it will decide everything.*

1911, Pedro Arrupe's parents Dolores Gondra Robles e Marcelino Arrupe Ugarte

1912, Pedro as a five year old boy

*1916, Pedro with his mother and sisters Isabel and Margarita at home in Bilbao*

*House where Arrupe was born, 7 Pelota Street, Bilbao, taken in 1987*

*1923, Arrupe in Bilbao*

*1924, Arrupe at Madrid School of Medicine*

*Lourdes in 1926, the year of Arrupe's visit*

*Lourdes around the time that Arrupe was to witness the miracles that inspired his vocation*

*1929, Pedro Arrupe at the end of his Jesuit novitiate*

*July 30, 1936, Fr. Pedro Arrupe's first Mass*

*1942, Arrupe as novice master in Yamaguchi, Japan*

*1942, The Novitiate in Yamaguchi, Japan*

*1944, Nagatsuka building in Hiroshima the year before the bomb*

*August 6, 1945, the day the atomic bomb fell on Hiroshima*

*August 6, 1945, the effects of the atomic bomb in Hiroshima*

*August 6, 1945, a victim of the atomic bomb in Hiroshima*

*August 9, 1945, the day the atomic bomb fell on Nagasaki*

*August 9, 1945, the effects of the atomic bomb felt in Nagasaki*

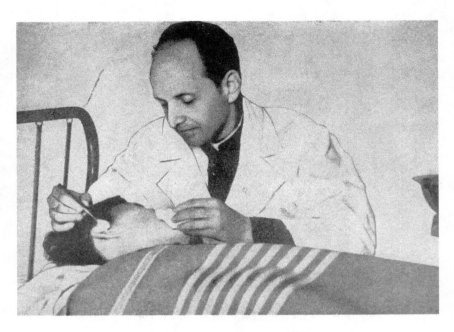

*August 10, 1945, Arrupe tending a bomb victim in Hiroshima*

*1954, Arrupe at his desk in Nagasaki*

1959, Provincial in Japan

1964, Arrupe with Dr. Ochoa, a former classmate, and a Nobel Prize winner.

1965, Papal audience shortly before being elected General

1966, visit to the USA, New Orleans

*1967, in center for orphans in India*

*1967, visit to India*

*1967, visit to school in India*

*1970, visit to Scotland*

*1971, visit to Loyola College, Baltimore, USA*

*1971, curbside greeting in Chicago, USA*

*1971, talks to scholastics, St. Louis, USA*

*1971, visit to Santa Clara USA*

*1971, visit to New York, USA, with Frs. Small and O'Keefe*

*1971, visit to New York, USA, a happy moment in the recreation room*

*1971, Arrupe meets shoeshine boy in Quito, Ecuador*

*1971, Arrupe meets shoeshine boy in Quito, Ecuador*

*1979, Fr. Arrupe is blessed by Pope John Paul II*

*1981, visit to Bangkok, his last visit abroad before falling ill*

*1981, Pope John Paul II visits the Jesuits*

*1982, audience with Pope John Paul II*

*1985, visit from Pope John Paul II*

*1985, visit from Mother Teresa of Calcutta*

9 780852 449691